Cambridge Elements ≡

Elements in the Philosophy of Ludwig Wittgenstein
edited by
David G. Stern
University of Iowa

WITTGENSTEIN ON MUSIC

Eran Guter
The Max Stern Yezreel Valley College

CAMBRIDGE
UNIVERSITY PRESS

Shaftesbury Road, Cambridge CB2 8EA, United Kingdom

One Liberty Plaza, 20th Floor, New York, NY 10006, USA

477 Williamstown Road, Port Melbourne, VIC 3207, Australia

314–321, 3rd Floor, Plot 3, Splendor Forum, Jasola District Centre,
New Delhi – 110025, India

103 Penang Road, #05–06/07, Visioncrest Commercial, Singapore 238467

Cambridge University Press is part of Cambridge University Press & Assessment,
a department of the University of Cambridge.

We share the University's mission to contribute to society through the pursuit of
education, learning and research at the highest international levels of excellence.

www.cambridge.org
Information on this title: www.cambridge.org/9781009500494

DOI: 10.1017/9781009313742

First published 2024

A catalogue record for this publication is available from the British Library.

ISBN 978-1-009-50049-4 Hardback
ISBN 978-1-009-31375-9 Paperback
ISSN 2632-7112 (online)
ISSN 2632-7104 (print)

Cambridge University Press & Assessment has no responsibility for the persistence
or accuracy of URLs for external or third-party internet websites referred to in this
publication and does not guarantee that any content on such websites is, or will
remain, accurate or appropriate.

Wittgenstein on Music

Elements in the Philosophy of Ludwig Wittgenstein

DOI: 10.1017/9781009313742
First published online: February 2024

Eran Guter
The Max Stern Yezreel Valley College
Author for correspondence: Eran Guter, erang@yvc.ac.il

Abstract: In this Element, the author set out to answer a twofold question concerning the importance of music to Wittgenstein's philosophical progression and the otherness of this sort of philosophical importance vis-à-vis philosophy of music as practiced today in the analytic tradition. The author starts with the idea of making music together and with Wittgenstein's master simile of language-as-music. The author traces these themes as they play out in Wittgenstein early, middle, and later periods. The author argues that Wittgenstein's overarching reorientation of the concept of depth pertaining to music in the aftermath of his anthropological turn, and against the backdrop of the outlook of German Romanticism, culminates in his unique view of musical profundity as "knowledge of people." This sets Wittgenstein's view in sharp contrast with certain convictions and debates that typify current analytically inclined philosophy of music.

This Element also has a video abstract: www.cambridge.org/Guter

Keywords: Wittgenstein, music, aesthetics, aspects, language

ISBNs: 9781009500494 (HB), 9781009313759 (PB), 9781009313742 (OC)
ISSNs: 2632-7112 (online), 2632-7104 (print)

Contents

Introduction

In 1949, two years before his untimely death, Ludwig Wittgenstein said to his friend Maurice O'Connor Drury regarding his current work on aspect-seeing: "It is impossible for me to say in my book one word about all that music has meant in my life. How then can I hope to be understood?" (Drury 2017, 136). This Element is an attempt to make philosophical sense of what Wittgenstein undeniably thought was the deepest connection between the experience and the life of music, and his philosophical progression.

As a research topic, Wittgenstein's remarks on music suffered prolonged neglect by both Wittgenstein scholars and philosophers of music. The former for a long time opted to consider them as subpar, insignificant, or otherwise irrelevant to the main body of Wittgenstein's philosophy and its evolution. The latter often sideline them, at least in the stronghold of contemporary analytic philosophy of music. For instance, Scruton (1999, viii) pointed out that Wittgenstein's writings "have little to say about the problems which I believe to be central to the discipline: the relationship between sound and tone, the analysis of musical meaning, and the nature of the purely musical experience." Similarly, Davies (2011, 298) observed that Wittgenstein "did not develop an account of music as such, or any systematic theory of aesthetics."

The last two decades have seen a steadily growing renewed interest in Wittgenstein's remarks on music and acknowledgment of their philosophical relevance and importance. The contribution of this Element is in its twofold purpose: not only to show how the musical examples, topics, and images he explored and investigated were used to test, refine, and develop his own philosophical views, but also to use the ensuing understanding of Wittgenstein's view on music as a foil to better appreciating his otherness as a philosopher of music, as he set himself to undo some gravitational forces that still pull together and shape current debates in analytically inclined philosophy of music. Hence, I would like to set myself apart from some distinct tendencies in the extant literature.

First, I avoid biographizing Wittgenstein's remarks on music. I see this as an exegetical pitfall, which may yield to a variety of causal fallacies in one's reading of the remarks.[1] Focusing primarily on Wittgenstein's preferred musical repertoire, his fondness of certain composers and dislike of others, his cultural upbringing as a child, or his personal habits does not guarantee in any way solid insight into, or justification of his philosophical thinking and its progression.

---

[1] Take for example Szabados's (2014, 41) claim that Hanslick's musical formalism influenced Wittgenstein's view on music in the *Tractatus* via "early nursery training" at the Wittgenstein Palais in Vienna. Such an argument runs the risk of begging the question.

In some cases, as it happens, it is even quite the contrary. For instance, Brahms, whose music Wittgenstein's adored, yet contrarily opted to associate his own movement of thought with the compositional free-spirit of Bruckner (Guter 2019a); or Mahler, whose music Wittgenstein despised, yet attributed philosophical importance to it (Guter 2015). Biographical details matter, but only as pointers for the inflection of a given remark, for the appropriate register for taking it in, not as a causal determinant for its justification, rigor, or upshot.

Second, I avoid starting from some broader programmatic commitment to one exegetical orthodoxy or another.[2] The merits of this kind of reading notwithstanding, it inevitably has the effect of a powerful filtering lens. It brings to the fore certain elements, while downplaying or sidelining others. Such a reading requires philosophical justification, which may be external to the corpus being interpreted, and full disclosure concerning the demarcation of the scope of the reading and its built-in limitations. I maintain that this kind of project shifts the focus away from the fine-grained textual embeddedness of the remarks on music, rendering them as serviceable means for a greater cause.

Third, for similar reasons, I avoid starting from standard gear analytic philosophy of music (concerning specialized topics such as ontology, expression, representation, etc.) and then trying to cast Wittgenstein's remarks on music in accordance with a philosophical tradition, whose most basic concepts, as Scruton (2004, 1) pointed out, "became articulated, during the twentieth century, in ways that were inimical to Wittgenstein's vision." If my goal in this Element is also to flesh out Wittgenstein's otherness as a philosopher of music, then his remarks on music must speak for themselves in their original philosophical occasion or context.

Finally, I am also not interested in the didactic exercise of starting from some interpretation of Wittgenstein's philosophical ideas or concepts (early or late) and then utilizing his remarks on music for the sake of generating a theorical angle in musicology or music theory, that is, approximating Wittgenstein's remarks on music to a body of knowledge pertaining somehow to a conceptual determination of the object "music." Such a tendency (mostly among musicologists who read Wittgenstein) once again shifts the focus away from the fine-grained textual embeddedness of Wittgenstein's remarks on music. I also find this sort of interpretation to be counter-intuitive. Despite his wealth of remarks on music and musicians in the *Nachlass*, Wittgenstein does not seem to hold a theory of music. Indeed, one would not expect him to devise such a theory, and it would be wrong to assume that what he says about music should be taken simply as the foundation of a systematic account of music.

---

[2] An excellent example is Appelqvist's (2023) reading of Wittgenstein as a thoroughbred Kantian.

Thus, I opt to start from a close reading of Wittgenstein's writing on music, as embedded in their respective context, seeing how they play out in his philosophy. Most of his remarks on music cannot be regarded as self-sufficient, and must be read in their original context, and more often than not, also against the appropriate texts and background ideas. The question of context becomes even more pressing from the perspective of musicology, music theory, and performance practice. While an attempt to glean from Wittgenstein's remarks on music a genuine insight into this or that musical piece might result in disappointment, it is nonetheless imperative to approach them from a musically informed standpoint. Some of his historically or technically confused remarks on music do have a point, which often proves to be philosophically important regardless of the status of their musicological soundness. In such cases, a musically informed context must be brought into the discussion in order to appreciate the point being made. Hence, when confronted with nonstandard use of technical terms or with what appears to be a musical prejudice, my interpretative method will be to see Wittgenstein's point in bringing up the issue in the given context rather than to accept it as is, hook, line, and sinker, or to dismiss it as being musically unsound.[3]

My discussion has both a systematic facet and a historical facet. In the first section I offer a systematic overview of underlying themes, which account for the importance of music for Wittgenstein's philosophizing. I start with the very idea of making music together, which also orients my ensuing discussion toward Wittgenstein's remarks on music, which fully engage his philosophical progression, and away from those which are mostly an occasion for him to merely voice his cultured taste, hence are secondary for my purpose here. I then set up the "stereoscopic" focal point of my argument by contrasting what I call the "music reproduction mechanisms axis" (concerning such devices as the gramophone, the pianola, and the music box) with the "language-as-music axis." The following three sections are historical, following the standard division between the early, the middle, and the late periods in Wittgenstein's philosophy, and there I aim to show how these underlying themes play out in the shapeshifting landscapes of Wittgenstein's philosophical progression. I offer a deflationary account of music in Wittgenstein's *Tractatus*, based on historical and textual evidence concerning his empirical research of the nature and importance of rhythm in music at the time before he began his work on the *Tractatus*. I then portray Wittgenstein's overarching reorientation of the concept of depth pertaining to music in the aftermath of his anthropological turn, and

---

[3] For concrete examples for my interpretative method, see the analysis of Wittgenstein's musical fragments in Guter and Guter (2023).

against the backdrop of the outlook of German Romanticism. Wittgenstein's complex, philosophically forward-looking response culminates in his own unique view of musical profundity in terms of what he calls "Menschenkenntnis" (knowing human beings). In the final, fifth section I offer my twofold answer to the double-edged question, which I posed in this introduction, concerning the importance of music to Wittgenstein's philosophical progression and the otherness of this sort of philosophical importance vis-à-vis convictions and debates that typify current analytically inclined philosophy of music.

1 Language as Music

1.1 Making Music Together

In a singular passage from a letter, which Wittgenstein wrote to his friend Rudolf Koder in 1930 (LK, 37–38), we encounter a candid disclosure of his primary attitude to music:

> The only possibility for getting to know a piece of music is indeed this: you play it and thereby notice distinctly that you play it and the passages still without understanding. You can then either not listen any further to these voices (inside you) and play the piece with no understanding as before, or listen to the voices, and then you will be prompted to play the appropriate passages again and again and, as it were, investigate. The less lazy you are, the further this will go, that is to say, the more passages will emerge for you as still not really felt. For the inner voices will be encouraged to speak by listening to them once, and more or less brought to silence by ignoring them. The more you listen the more you will hear, and voices that would have been hardly audible at first will then speak more and more distinctly and new ones will turn up. Before that, the laziness of every man shies one away and one has the feeling: as soon as I let in for these voices, who knows where they could eventually bring me. And yet one can only say: listen carefully and follow what it says to you, and you will see, you will then hear more and more distinctly, and you will know more and more about yourself.[4]

This passage broaches topics and themes that will repeatedly show up in the following sections under various interconnected guises and contexts. First and foremost, the primacy of playing, that "dance of human fingers" on the piano keyboard (CV, 42 [36]), and the actual phrasing and rephrasing of a passage in order to characterize it. Yet also the realization that a certain phrasing and characterization of a certain passage may elude me; the investigative nature of making such comparisons; the daring choice to take on a specific phrasing as an

---

[4] My translation.

invitation to traverse a whole field of possibilities, enabling meaningful distinctions between right and wrong, in hope of reaching one that would necessitate itself, to see in the score something I had not seen before; the richness of character which ensues from such traversing and the sense of deepening as an articulation of possibilities that serves and instances further possibilities for characterization of what may be heard. And, finally, most importantly, what such deepening can teach me about myself, how phrasing and characterizing change me in return – there is always a choice to be made, an effort is required, indeed, even courage is called for.

As Hagberg (2017, 73) points out, Wittgenstein recovers in his writing on music "a full-blooded sense of practice-focused embodiment against the abstractions of a disembodied idealism (of a kind that, given the inducements of certain linguistic forms, remain ever-present in aesthetics)." Importantly, one such abstraction is the entrenched idea of "the musical work" as has been traditionally set against the idea of "the musical event." Wittgenstein's (CV, 60 [52]) notion of an interaction (*Wechselwirkung*) between music and language[5] is geared toward a conception of music (and language) as a deed, as something that people do, as an ever-open invitation to learn, listen and play.[6] It recovers the sense in which playing music is not merely subservient to the musical work. Rather, musical works are there for us to play, for ourselves, for others, and, most importantly, with others.

Apart from certain well-demarcated remarks, in which Wittgenstein primarily gives voice to his cultured taste in composers and musical repertoire, the philosophical focal point in many of his more textually integrated passages on music is the kind of mindful human encounter that is captured by that inviting German verb *musizieren* – "Mindless speaking and speaking which is not mindless," says Wittgenstein (MS 129, 115), "are to be compared to mindless music making (*musizieren*) and music making which is not mindless."[7] The passage from the letter to Koder exemplifies the latter, sought-after case. Here the idea of musical understanding displaces that of musical meaning.[8] For Wittgenstein, we can have no idea what musical meaning might be unless we have some grasp of what distinguishes the one who hears with understanding from the one who merely hears. This is the crux of the notion of musicality,[9] which, I will argue in the next section, has established itself as a philosophical

---

[5] I discuss this further in Section 4.   [6] Cf. BB, 166.

[7] Wittgenstein alternates between "playing a musical piece" and "making music." All references to Wittgenstein's *Nachlass* are to *Wittgenstein Source* (WS). All translations from the *Nachlass* are mine, unless indicated otherwise. All other quotations from Wittgenstein conform to the print editions, as specified in the list of references at the end of this Element. Modifications of these quotations are flagged by a footnote.

[8] See Scruton (2004).   [9] See LC, I:17.

driving force for Wittgenstein from the very beginning of his career, strikingly even before the time of the *Tractatus*.

This brings to the fore an idea, which is best captured in Schütz's (1951) phrase "mutual tuning-in relationships."[10] According to Schütz (1951, 96–97), this relationship, which is exemplified in making music together,

> is established by the reciprocal sharing of the other's flux of experiences in inner time, by living through a vivid present together, by experiencing this togetherness as a "We". Only within this experience does the other's conduct become meaningful to the partner tuned in on him – that is, the other's body and its movements can be and are interpreted as a field of expression of events within his inner life.

Such reciprocity "is bound to an occurrence in the outer world, which has the structure of a series of events [which are embodied in facial expressions, gait, posture, ways of handling instruments etc.] polythetically built up in outer time" (Schütz 1951, 97).

The importance of mutual tuning-in relationships for Wittgenstein is best captured in his occasional explicit probing into the idea of musical simultaneity, searching for the "musical now," without which there can be no making music together, and as a matter of fact, there can be no music as we normally understand the term.[11] I argued elsewhere (Guter 2019b) that Wittgenstein's emphasis on mutual tuning-in relationships shows clearly in his middle-period reversal of Augustine's prioritizing of memory-time in his account of the specious present (famously couched in musical terms in Augustine's *Confessions*). Wittgenstein subsumed memory-time under what he called "information time" – the order of events, involving the specification of time-references by means of public, observable chronology, which is implemented not only by means of chronometers and calendars, but also, and more importantly, by means of consulting other people, as well as documents, diaries, manuscripts, and other modes of making records and structuring narratives. In order not to fall prey to the image of musical experience as a kind of, say, seashell that everyone carries with him close to his ear, and to the corresponding specter of a metaphysical owner for each such seashell, we must acknowledge that our utterances about our musical experiences, if they are to be used meaningfully, must rely on the framework of our ordinary language.

Relying on the order of "information time" in music involves the innumerous, multiform specific ways of characterizing all that is there is to behold when

---

[10] The title of this section is a nod to Schütz's seminal essay.
[11] See e.g., CV 85 [75], 92 [80 – the transcription here is wrong; hence the English translation is misleading].

we make music together, rendering our musicality manifest, including the experience of musical motion through rhythm and structure, the identification and re-identification of musical materials, the fine nuances of musical expression, and the overarching considerations of performance practice, of genre and style. Wittgenstein's own examples broach this broad scope of musicality: hearing a theme as a march or as a dance;[12] hearing a certain bar as an introduction or in a certain key;[13] experiencing a certain interpretation of a musical passage as inevitable;[14] playing a passage with more intense or with less intense expressiveness, with either stronger or lesser emphasis on rhythm and structure;[15] playing a passage with the correct sort of expression;[16] hearing one thing as a variant of another;[17] rephrasing a variation in such a way that it could be conceived as a different variation on the same theme, hearing a theme differently in a repetition;[18] hearing a melody differently after becoming acquainted with the composer's style.[19]

For Wittgenstein, these are all examples of aspect perception.[20] They all pertain unequivocally to ways in which "character" in music is drawn: timbre, dynamics, balance, articulation, tempo, beat division, and rhythmic flexibility. All of them prominently exhibit not only the primacy of playing in giving rise to the said experience, but also its ineliminably open-ended investigative character in one's attempt to find the right balance of elements, as Wittgenstein underscored in his letter to Koder. According to Floyd (2018a, 368), characterizing involves "the 'coming into view' of a scheme of possibilities available for characterization given a particular mode of characterization." We patently need to seek the right level and arrangement of elements in order to reveal something, to discover ways in which possibilities are revealed and may necessitate themselves. The tentative phrase "inner voices" in Wittgenstein's letter can be replaced by the logical notion of possibility. For Wittgenstein, aspects are precisely spaces of possibilities that are there to be perceived. In this sense, where Wittgenstein says in the letter that the more one listens to these

---

[12] PPF §209 [PI, xi, 206]. I use the 2009 edition of the *Philosophical Investigations* throughout this Element. References to "Philosophy of Psychology: A Fragment" (PPF), which used to be known as Part II of *Philosophical Investigations*, are cited from both the 2009 and 1958 editions. References to the latter are given in square brackets.

[13] RPPI §; Z §208.   [14] RPPI §22.   [15] RPPI §507.   [16] LWI §688.

[17] RPPI § 508; RPPII §494.   [18] RPPI §517.   [19] LWI §774.

[20] These, and many other of Wittgenstein's musical examples for aspect perception, far exceed the import of his onetime duck-rabbit example (PPF §128 [PI, xi, 194]), which is commonly referred to in the literature as a paradigmatic case. I agree with Baz (2000, 100) that focusing on the duck-rabbit example is philosophically misleading, since it is simply not typical of aspects that they "will come in pairs, and that most people will be able to see the two, and to flip back and forth between them at will. It is also not typical of aspects that they will be elicited from us as part of a psychological experiment or a philosophical illustration." See also Cavell (1979, 354ff).

"inner voices" the more one hears, and "voices" that would have been hardly audible at first will then speak more and more distinctly and new ones will turn up, he was actually making a general point about aspects. In Floyd's (2018a, 366) words, "with success, the 'face' of what is characterized shines through in a comprehensible and communicable way, affording us ways to see likenesses and differences, and ways to go on discussing and drawing out from the articulation further aspects of what is characterized that are there to be seen in and by means of it." Wittgenstein's point to Koder in the letter is that success requires a choice to enter a mutual tuning-in relationship – that is, to play and listen, even for oneself[21] – and that this task is patently open-ended.

This sort of seeking out intimacy brings up another important point about aspects in contradistinction to cases in which we describe objects of perception in order to inform others of something, which for whatever reasons they cannot perceive by themselves, and whose perceived features are supposed to be independent of one's experience of it. Such language games of informing do not necessitate any form of intimacy. By contrast, when attempting to share an aspect, the other person needs to be there so she can trace my characterization. Perceiving the object for what it is (a visual configuration or a progression of tones) is not the issue, but rather characterizing what possibilities are there (a smile, or an answer to a previous passage, which we would characterize as a question). In such cases, whatever we do to give voice to the perceiving of the aspect, to enable the other person to share the aspect with us, says Wittgenstein (RPPI §874), is not offered "to inform the other person," but rather to "find one another" (*sich finden*).[22] As Baz (2020, 6) says, appreciating aspects "makes for a particular type of opportunity for seeking intimacy with others, or putting it to the test." Availing myself of Schütz's (1951) words, I may say that, for Wittgenstein, as we open up to further characterizations in music, we experience this togetherness intimately as a "We."

Wittgenstein's final striking remark in the passage from his letter to Koder connects the idea of investigative characterization with our ability to know human beings (ourselves and others), to see the face of the human. This places Wittgenstein's remarks on music also in the context of the history of ideas as pertaining to conceptualizing the profundity of the art of music. This is his take on a venerable Romantic theme, which is encapsulated in Wackenroder's (1971, 191) words, "the human heart becomes acquainted with itself in the mirror of

---

[21] Schütz (1951) argues that mutual tuning-in relationships obtain also when we listen to a recording of music or even when one attends to music in one's mind.

[22] In the print edition, *sich finden* is translated as "being in touch with one another." I find this unnecessarily cumbersome, certainly when used in the first person.

musical sounds." Wittgenstein reworked and gradually interweaved this conception of musical profundity into his forward thinking about the philosophic entanglements of language and the mind.[23]

1.2 Gramophones, Pianolas, and Music Boxes

Allusions to mechanical means of musical reproduction appear regularly in Wittgenstein's writings from the *Tractatus* to his late-vintage, post-*Philosophical Investigations* texts. They comprise an important distinct axis in Wittgenstein's philosophical progression for the seemingly improbable reason that they are all unmusical. Yet, that is their point, and therein lies their philosophical purpose. I find it useful to bracket them here as a foil to Wittgenstein's notion of musicality, which is at the center of this Element.

We first encounter the gramophone at the very heart of the *Tractatus* (TLP 4.014–4.0141) as part of an analogy, which Wittgenstein employs to introduce his picture theory. The analogy is supposed to elucidate Wittgenstein's idea that language stands in an internal relation of depicting to the world. The odd fact that the gramophone epitomizes Wittgenstein's treatment of music at the time of the *Tractatus* introduces an anomaly into the trajectory of his thinking about music, which I will tackle head-on in the next section. For now, it will be instructive to point out that Wittgenstein himself acknowledged that the gramophone is not musical precisely in the sense that I explored in the previous section. Drury (2017, 44–45) reports an occasion on which listening together with Wittgenstein to a recording of Pablo Casals playing the cello led to a discussion on how recording technology had improved from their days together in Cambridge with the arrival of long-play records. Wittgenstein's comment was that "it is so characteristic that, just when the mechanics of reproduction are so vastly improved, there are fewer and fewer people who know how the music should be played."

Many of Wittgenstein's allusions to the gramophone have nothing to do with music, but rather with the reproduction of speech, where the evocation of technology is supposed to underscore the mechanical uncanniness of speaking without thinking. The parrot often joins the gramophone in these remarks.[24] Perhaps the most appropriate image of the gramophone as Wittgenstein came to realize it in his later writings – "Imagine that instead of a stone you were transformed into a gramophone" (MS 165, 7) – is found in a hilarious passage from James Joyce's (2000, 141) *Ulysses*:

---

[23] This will be the subject matter of my discussion in Sections 3 and 4.
[24] See, e.g., PI §344; RPPI §496; Z §396; MS165, 209f; TS 242a, 180f; MS 136, 51a; MS 136, 78a f.

> Besides how could you remember everybody? Eyes, walk, voice. Well, the voice, yes: gramophone. Have a gramophone in every grave or keep it in the house. After dinner on a Sunday. Put on poor old greatgrandfather. Kraahraark! Hellohellohello amawfullyglad kraark awfullygladaseeagain hellohello amawf krpthsth. Remind you of the voice like the photograph reminds you of the face.

This caricature, complete with an irrepressible allure of later-Wittgensteinian ridicule as directed at his onetime picture theory, nonetheless captures a thought which is evinced in the few other remarks where the allusion to the gramophone touches upon music.

On one occasion (BB, 40), Wittgenstein evokes the allusion to the gramophone in the context of discussing cases of sudden understanding, for instance, when we know how to continue whistling a tune that we know very well, after it was interrupted in the middle. "It might appear as though the whole continuation of the tune had to be present while I knew how to go on," Wittgenstein says (BB, 40). A series of questions arises: What sort of process is this *knowing how to go on*? How long does it take to know how to go on? Is it an instantaneous process? Wittgenstein is concerned with the tendency to mystify the word "thought" by assuming that there must be some extremely accelerated inner process that runs in the background of our mind, as if the whole thought and its future development must be contained in an instant.[25] The justification for this conviction, when we suddenly understand how to continue the tune, is closely related to Wittgenstein's discussion of following a rule. When we are prompted to discuss the speed of thought (e.g., when a thought flashes through our head or a solution to a problem becomes clear), there is a tendency to uphold a separation between the thought qua inner process and its overt expression.

Wittgenstein uses the allusion to the gramophone to jam this tendency. His point is that we would be making the mistake of mixing up the existence of a gramophone record of a tune with the existence of the tune, if we assume that whenever a tune passes through existence there must be some sort of a gramophone record of it from which it is played. Here, as in related remarks, Wittgenstein's upshot was that we recognize that the circumstances justifying the conviction that one knows how to continue with the tune have nothing to do with something peculiar occurring in one's mind; instead, one's conviction is justified by one's past training and performance – by what one is capable of doing.[26] Yet there is a further point about the distinction between the existence of a gramophone record of a tune (a matter of storage) and the existence of the tune (a matter of playing it through correctly). The tune as archived in the

---

[25] Cf. PI §§318–20.   [26] See the analysis of Figure 1 in Guter and Guter (2023).

gramophone record is complete in the sense that it is repeatable without error or decay and without location. It is also not doomed to dwindle from a presence to a mere impression and wear away as its performance fades into memory. This is equally true also of the voice of poor old great-grandfather. Yet with respect to music, this completeness leaves no room for all that could go wrong in performance, for the feat of improvising impromptu, as Goehr (2016) calls it. Kramer (2012, 131–132) points out that "the idealizing effect of the gramophone depends on foreclosing uncertainty. The recorded performance is not simply over but *safely* over." For Wittgenstein, musicality importantly inheres in a risk of loss and error which cannot be archived by the technology. Presumably, this is also the point in Wittgenstein's comment to Drury that the technological progress in the mechanics of musical reproduction does not allow for knowing how the music should be played – for that calls for knowing and appreciating the embodied incompleteness of making music.

A similar point is evoked on another occasion (BB, 184), when Wittgenstein offers Schumann's piano piece "Wie aus weiter Ferne" (as from the distance) from *Davidsbündlertänze* Op. 6 as an example for a gesture of pastness. He then suggests (for the sake of argument) to consider a gramophone recording of a successfully expressive rendition of the piece as "the most elaborate and exact expression of a feeling of pastness that I can imagine." Of course, Wittgenstein's example is one of cultured taste – arguably poor old great-grandfather's holler from the gramophone "awfullygladaseeagain hellohello" may come across "wie aus weiter Ferne" equally well. Be that as it may, in both cases the sound of the (right) expression has been safely stored and we can retrieve it repeatably risk- and error-free. Yet in the context of Wittgenstein's discussion on this occasion, this sort of mechanical encapsulation once again serves to flesh out an anomaly: a tendency to imagine a disembodied distillation of "an amorphous something in a place, the mind" – as if we could render the (musical) expression of the feeling of pastness in separation from its being enacted and embodied in our human environment, that is, in separation from gesture.

A direct line connects the gramophone to Wittgenstein's recurrent allusions to the pianola.[27] Whereas in the gramophone there is a needle tracking the grooves of the surface of the record, in the pianola there is a mechanism of pegs which tracks the pattern of perforation in the pianola roll and operates the piano hammers accordingly. Both the gramophone and the pianola are universal reading machines in the sense that the mechanism is capable of reading off anything as long as it is set in the appropriate physical medium.[28] In both cases,

---

[27] See, e.g., PG, 69–70; BB, 118–120; PI §157.

[28] One is reminded of Rilke's (1961) suggestion to track the coronal suture of a human skull with a gramophone needle in order to release its primal sound.

the physical medium is finitely and safely encoded and the (correct) operation of the mechanism guarantees repeatable playback, which is risk- and error-free. Wittgenstein used the pianola example exclusively (in his middle- to late-periods) to explicate his ideas about rule following. Presumably, the overt mechanical robustness of the pianola, say its dumbness, suited this purpose perfectly. Wittgenstein's point is that the pianola is the perfect model for being guided by signs. The combination of perforations on the pianola roll is an order, or a command that guides the mechanism to yield a certain result.

Wittgenstein's focus here is on the concept of "reading," which is to be understood primarily as correctly reproducing in speech the sounds that are associated with the words on a page. The question that Wittgenstein poses concerns the difference between someone who reads and someone who merely pretends to read. He evokes the pianola in the context of exploring the case of a person who is a "reading machine." We are asked to imagine someone who is trained to produce the right sounds on seeing the written signs, whether or not he understands those signs. Importantly, in a case like this, understanding is patently dropped out of consideration for the sake of argument.[29] The pianola analogy allows Wittgenstein to flesh out the mentalist tendency to think of language in terms of a psychological mechanism. His point is that the one who reads (as opposed to one who merely pretends to read), derives what he says from the text, yet either way this does not depend on anything which went through one's mind at the time of the reading, but rather on what one is capable of doing with the text. Just like with the gramophone and the sudden understanding of how to continue whistling a well-known tune (BB, 40), reading is the exercise of an ability, not a manifestation of a mechanism (mental or biological).[30] The text is not the cause, but rather the reason for reading in a certain way.

This is precisely where the overt mechanics of the pianola (as a reading machine) epitomizes the sense of being unmusical as a foil for Wittgenstein's treatment of the concept of understanding, which he sees as being linked in complex ways with one's participation in a characteristic form of life. "When I understand a sentence," says Wittgenstein (PG, 72), "something happens like

---

[29] It is noteworthy that Wittgenstein (PI §156) opts to extend this notion of reading as to include also "playing by notes" (*nach Noten zu spielen*). This is not the same, I take it, as playing from a score (which is how the phrase has usually been translated, misleadingly I believe). Playing from a score (professional sight reading, reading figured bass, etc.) is precisely the kind of reading with understanding, which is contrary to Wittgenstein's purpose in considering the case of the human "reading machine." Playing by notes, quite literally (I suggest), where these consist solely of, say, values of pitch and duration, would fit in the present context. Cf. Wittgenstein's (PG, 191) own example for making a pupil into a "playing-machine."

[30] See the analysis of Figure 2 in Guter and Guter (2023).

being able to follow a melody as a melody." According to Schoenberg (1999, 102), "a melody can be compared to an 'aperçu,' an 'aphorism,' in its rapid advance from problem to solution." A melody is independent and self-determined – it requires no addition, continuation, or elaboration – and it seeks to reestablish repose through balance. It should exhibit a sense of cohesiveness (otherwise it may just sound like a broken chord) and continuity. Most importantly, it is bound to achieve a sense of closure (by means of tonal organization and compositional syntax), of coming back home. To follow a melody *as a melody* means that we need to characterize what we hear as a melody. According to Wittgenstein, this could be done in a multitude of ways, manifested within facial expressions, gestures, the comparisons drawn, and the images chosen to illustrate that understanding, or indeed simply the particular way in which a person plays or hums the piece in question (CV, 80 [70]). Yet all such characterizations presuppose "familiarity with conclusions, confirmations, replies, etc." (CV, 59 [52]), as well as (one could add) with tensions and resolutions, repose and balance, directedness, closures, and a sense of home. That is, our characterizations impinge upon an indefinite edifice of innumerous interrelated language games, which ultimately run the gamut of "the whole field of our language games" (CV, 59 [52]).[31] As Hagberg (2017, 92) puts it, they occur "within our cultivated sensibilities and imagination-assisted perception, within the stream of musical life." In this sense, for Wittgenstein, musicality underscores his thrust (throughout his middle and later philosophical work) to show that the grammar of the concept of understanding traverses the topography of our practices and connects it with the complex and involved filigree patterns of our form of life.

Against this backdrop, we also encounter Wittgenstein's allusions to music boxes (*Spieluhrmusik*). Compared to the pianola, music boxes are not even universal reading machines. They are built in such a way as to produce a mechanically stiff rendition of a severely limited, fixed musical repertoire, so everything about their repeating playback quickly becomes totally predictable, at some point even ad nauseam. Thus, they stand in stark contrast to the indefiniteness of our mutual tuning-in relationships and our ability to characterize. "This musical phrase is a gesture for me. It creeps into my life. I make it my own," says Wittgenstein (CV, 83 [73]), and continues to explain, "Life's infinite variations are essential to our <u>life</u> in incalculability." Of course, everything about the playback of a music box is completely calculable and predictable. Yet, says Wittgenstein (CV, 84 [73]), "Its gestures would still remain gestures for me

---

[31] I return to this subject in Section 4.2.

although I know all the time, what comes next. Indeed I may even be surprised afresh again & again. (In a certain sense.)"[32]

Wittgenstein uses the allusion to the unmusical music box to point out that our musical ability to tune-in on the music box and render its gestures as meaningful, to make them our own, hinges upon "the habitual character of life," to wit, our form of life, when what we hear anew as a gesture pertains to what Wittgenstein elsewhere (LWI §211) calls "patterns of life," expressive regularities that emerge from persistent, though constantly varied, repetition.[33] The natural foundation of patterns of live is the complex nature and the variety of human contingencies. Wittgenstein makes a similar point when he suggests that we try to imagine "other beings" that might recognize soulful expression in music by rules (RPPII §695; Z §157). Wittgenstein explicitly says (Z §164) that the idea of "culture" is needed to explain what expressive playing is. His point again is that "to understand a piece of music means to understand music as a whole, as a culture-wide, practice-embedded complex of phenomena" (Hagberg 2017, 92). Wittgenstein's (RPPII §696) thought experiment, where he asks us to imagine discovering people who knew only the music of music boxes, is designed to show that musical expression is constituted in such a way that an encounter with such a mechanical surrogate for expression would have a petrifying effect.

The problem has nothing to do with the mechanism of music boxes – the fact that one can predict exactly what they play and how they play it – but with the possibility that such imagined music is grammatically related to a rigid, fixed, definite physiognomy recognizable only by exact rules. In such imagined music, indeterminacy implies a deficiency in knowledge – there is no (conceptual) room for the moment of finding one another. The point is that this is not the case of musical expression as we know it, even in the case of music boxes.

1.3 The Master Simile

In the remarks which I discussed so far, and in those I discuss in the following sections, what Wittgenstein says about music interacts with what he wants to say about language. This is very typical of him. In fact, as I pointed out in my introduction, if there is a major frustration with Wittgenstein among analytic philosophers of music, it is because there is nothing in Wittgenstein's multifarious remarks on music that comes even close to outlining a "philosophy of

---

[32] Cf. RFM II §3ff. Wittgenstein uses the analogy with music to make a similar point about being surprised in the case of a mathematic puzzle. His emphasis is on the importance and the pleasure of active arrangement of concepts and symbols, and open-ended self-discovery, which allow us to expand, rearrange, and interpret our expressive powers. See Floyd (2010).

[33] I return to this subject in Section 4.3.

music" understood as an attempt to conceptually determine the object "music." For Wittgenstein, the discourse on both music and language is ineliminably circumscribed within the realm of language as a universal medium. It is important, however, to spell out the nature of the relation between music and language in Wittgenstein's thinking. Wittgenstein developed early on what I would call a "master simile," comparing language to music. The direction of the simile, thinking of language as music (rather than vice versa), is philosophically potent. It involves seeking out sensibilities and possibilities – the attending to voices, if you will – that pertain to, are imaginable through, or enhanced by making music together, and thus also a release from the need to be held captive by certain pictures of language. This is where thinking about music becomes intermingled with Wittgenstein's philosophical progression, rather than merely encapsulated as something that the great philosopher had to say about music at some point.

It always comes to me as a surprise to see other writers on the subject referring to Wittgenstein, even *en passant*, as if he was philosophically invested somehow in considering music as a language. On occasions, Wittgenstein refers to "phenomena with speech-like character in music and architecture" (CV, 40 [34]) or points out that "there is a strongly musical element in verbal language" (Z §161). He says that Bach's music, or something like the double bass recitative in the fourth movement of Beethoven's *Ninth* symphony, is more like language, than what we could find in Mozart or Haydn (CV, 40 [34]) and points out the unusual importance that people seem to have attached to the way in which Josef Labor's organ playing was reminiscent of speaking (CV, 71 [62]). However, nothing in such random remarks could substantiate the general claim that Wittgenstein tended to think of music as a language. These musical phenomena are quite clearly aspects of certain types or genres of music, or aspects of certain manners of performing music – a way of characterizing what we hear in terms of "significant irregularity" (CV, 40 [34]), that is, a way of drawing in significance.

Even when Wittgenstein says explicitly that "understanding a musical phrase may also be called understanding a *language*" (Z §172),[34] this needs to be read in context, where Wittgenstein refers to "the way music speaks" (Z §160) and reminds us that just like in the case of poetry we could say that music is perhaps

---

[34] This claim, taken in isolation, clearly makes good musicological sense when considering common-practice era music. It also coheres with Wittgenstein's contention that the musical theme interacts with language and becomes a new part of our language (CV, 59–60 [52]), which I discuss in Section 4. But this singular claim, I submit, cannot be taken as approximating something like Cooke's (1964) idea of devising a "musical lexicon" which would specify the emotive meaning of the basic units of the language of music, or like Lerdahl and Jackendoff's (1983) Chomskian attempt to devise a generative grammar for music.

composed in the language of information, but it is not used in the language-game of informing. The point again is that we may find one another within the culturally embedded, embodied provenance of our mutual tuning-in relation-ships. Otherwise, Wittgenstein pokes fun at the alternative (Z §161), "mightn't we imagine a person who, never having had any acquaintance with music, comes to us and hears someone playing a reflective piece of Chopin and is convinced that this is a language and people merely want to keep the meaning secret from him?"

The language-as-music simile appears as a distinct axis in Wittgenstein's philosophical progression, which runs parallel to and mirrors the one concern-ing his various allusions to mechanical means of musical reproduction, which I discussed in the previous section. In the early period it takes the form of a comparison between a sentence and a melody in terms of structure (NB, 41), which is then reworked into the *Tractatus* (TLP, 3.141), culminating in the gramophone analogy (TLP, 4.014–4.0141). In the middle period it takes the form of comparing understanding a sentence to understanding a melody or a theme in music (WVC, 395; PG, 72; BB, 167ff), which is carried over to his later period, featuring prominently in *Philosophical Investigations* (PI §527ff), where Wittgenstein initiates an intense discussion of aspects in language and the experience of meaning, which continues well into his late-vintage writings on the philosophy of psychology, including the framing of the idea of aspect- and meaning-blindness in terms of lacking a musical ear (PPF §260 [PI, xi, 214]).

Importantly, the language-as-music simile covers the fundamental physio-gnomic simile of "aspect in logic as a face" – comparing between logical features of what we say ("internal" or "formal" relations among these) and facial features, aspects of a human face that wears a certain look (happiness, grief, etc.) – which, as Floyd (2018a) argues, Wittgenstein developed early on in attempt to refashion Russell's notion of acquaintance. With this physiognomic simile Wittgenstein returned Russellian acquaintance to its everyday home, the sense in which we may be acquainted with a person. To be acquainted with a face, some mode of characterization – verbal or gestural or otherwise – must go on, the entering of a field of valence and possibility and contrast. Characterization draws in significance, reveals something, in a specific way using what Floyd calls "charactery" (e.g., letters of the alphabet, musical notes, facial features, expressions, gestures, colors of costumes, or elements of a formal system of logic). When we characterize, we envision certain charactery as specifically put together into a specific dimension of possibility. Getting to the particularity of that which is characterized, that is, rendering a physiognomy distinct, requires attending carefully to the specific way and manner of its characterization, and in particular, to the relevant system(s) of possibilities in which it inheres (Floyd 2018a).

Wittgenstein's growing emphasis on specific techniques of characterization and their embeddedness in a form of life, and with it the blooming of these two "sister similes" in his writings, are related to the anthropological turn in Wittgenstein's philosophy, which sets in in the aftermath of the *Tractatus*, beginning in the early 1930s.[35] This is already eminently clear in the passage from Wittgenstein's 1930 letter to Koder, which opened this section. Seeing a new possibility for phrasing a musical passage requires one to become acquainted with an aspect through the specific way and manner in which we phrase the score in the characterization. The very allusion to "voices" in Wittgenstein's letter is telling, because a voice can have character, no less than a face; it involves listening and responding. A voice calls out for characterization. The allusion to faces, facial features, and facial expression is quite standard in Wittgenstein's remarks on music, and it is typical of his discussion of aspects.[36]

The striking fact that music is constantly connected with aspects in Wittgenstein's thinking (even at the time before the *Tractatus*, as I argue in the next section) suggests a clue about how to read aspects in the later work through the eyes of the articulation of genuinely musical characteristics and meaningful characteristics of thought in language. On the reading, which I follow here, aspects in Wittgenstein's are taken without aestheticizing the notion of aspects, making it fundamental to all of Wittgenstein's later thoughts about language rather than something which pertains merely to aesthetics or to the philosophy of mind, as it is usually read.

2 The Early Period: Eliding Musicality

2.1 In Myers's Laboratory

I begin my discussion of Wittgenstein's early period at a point which is almost a decade before the publication of the *Tractatus*. To the best of my knowledge, all other writers on the subject reach as early as Wittgenstein's first written remarks on music, which he penned down in 1915 in his *Notebooks 1914–1916* (NB). However, my discussion begins even earlier with Wittgenstein's stint during the years 1912–1913 as a researcher at Charles S. Myers's laboratory for experimental psychology in Cambridge, where Wittgenstein eagerly conducted experiments on rhythm designed "to investigate [the] nature of rhythm" (WLM, 9:40) or otherwise "to ascertain the extent and importance of rhythm in music"

---

[35] I discuss this in Section 3.   [36] See the analysis of Figure 4 in Guter and Guter (2023).

(Pinsent 1990, 3). Undoubtedly, this is one of the least understood and often overlooked episodes in Wittgenstein's early period. Yet this was his earliest recorded engagement in thinking about music, not just appreciating it, and philosophizing by means of musical thinking. Most pertinent to our concerns here, this is also the earliest evidence we have of Wittgenstein's career-long exploration of the philosophically pervasive implications of mutual tuning-in relationships and noticing an aspect.

Wittgenstein's experiments concerned a phenomenon then called "subjective rhythm," aiming to determine the conditions under which subjects heard or read into a sequence of beats a rhythm which, in a sense, was not there.[37] The experiments followed Myers's protocol for laboratory exercise number 144 from the second volume of Myers's *Text-Book of Experimental Psychology, with Laboratory Exercises* (1911) almost to the letter, and they were carried out under the supervision of Myers, who took the experiments quite seriously.[38] Consistent with Myers's protocol, Wittgenstein (WLM, 9:41–42) reported that his subjects tended to group the beat train into groups of three, and to hear an accent on the first beat in each group. They also tended not to hear two consecutive beats as accentuated. Most interestingly, they experienced a conflict between tendencies to hear an accented pulse, a sort of "constant stumbling," when he tweaked the pulse train (WLM, 9:42).

Wittgenstein's later indifference to the scientific results of these experiments, and his ensuing general dissatisfaction with the use and abuse of the methods of experimental psychology for aesthetics notwithstanding,[39] this early episode is crucially significant when viewed in the context of Wittgenstein's thinking about music and its relation to his imminent philosophical progression. I argued (Guter 2020) that the striking thing about those experiments on rhythm is the fact that Wittgenstein probed into what he would later call "noticing an aspect." The mechanical apparatus for the experiments produced a sonic equivalent of an ambiguous figure. Wittgenstein's test subject could have heard the isochronal and equitonal pulse train either as duple meter or as triple meter (as was in fact the case in Wittgenstein's experiments), and they could have flipped back and forth between the two rhythmic patterns at will. This is specified in Myers's *Textbook*, including the tendency of the subjects to rephrase

---

[37] This phenomenon was already well documented and studied at the time. See, e.g., Bolton (1894), Wundt (1903), and Woodrow (1909).

[38] See Myers (2013), 98–99 and 301–302. Wittgenstein tweaked the original protocol by adding some elements taken from exercise no. 145 which concerns the perception of "objective rhythm." See my comparison between Myers's protocols and Wittgenstein's description of the experiments in Guter (2023b). For other descriptions of these experiments, see McGuinness (1988, 125–129) and Monk (1990, 49–50).

[39] See WLM, 9:40–42; LC, III:1–11.

certain unsustainable rhythmic patterns into other patterns, which accent the first beat.[40] So it stands to reason that Wittgenstein was well aware of this onset for aspect perception while designing his experiments, in particular regarding the added component of rhythmic manipulation.

Furthermore, and equally important, in the dynamic context of the experiments Wittgenstein sought after the ways of characterization in which noticing an aspect feeds back into the subjects' use of language, that is, after the communicability of aspects. His interest in the tuning-in of his test subjects on the mechanical pulse train anticipated his much later similar invocation of one's ability to tune-in on the predictable mechanical playing of a music box, which I discussed in the previous section.[41] Indeed, this was the source of the failure of these experiments, in Wittgenstein's eyes, but also the source of their significance for his philosophical development. The manner of characterizing, namely, the ability to give reasons for why significance is drawn in, was the real issue in his interrogation of his test subjects. Wittgenstein clearly says in retrospect that to answer the question about significance, to give a reason, requires making comparisons and ordering, as we draw in a field of possibilities and necessities, eventually offering the gift of a good simile. By his own admission (WLM, 9:40), he was looking for that in the experiments and he did not get that from many of his test subjects. "I was looking forward to talking with my subjects about something which interested me," Wittgenstein (WLM, 9:40–41) told his students years later, "I was looking for utterances inside an aesthetic system. [...] When I made those experiments, what would have satisfied me was comparison, within a system."

The experiments harbored an important philosophical lesson that "simple material" – such as the noticing of an aspect in the pulse train, characterized rhythmically – is not absolute. What is taken to be simple within one procedure or way of looking at things may wind up as being complex. The simple is not absolute, either as a fixed point of departure or as a fixed destination, but rather is relative to a choice of system. The philosophical shortcomings of these early experiments taught Wittgenstein that a touchstone of musical simplicity may come to look like a possible step in a journey, a starting point that we can share, break off from, pass off to the next person, reject, discuss, and contest. For Wittgenstein, engaging in mutual tuning-in was the embodiment of musicality.

2.2 Stumpf's Lasting Influence

Wittgenstein's experiments on rhythm ought to be situated in the context of Myers's research agenda at the time. Myers's laboratory was deeply invested in

---

[40] See Myers (2013), 302.   [41] See Section 1.2.

the study of musicality as manifested in tone judgment. There was significant ethnological emphasis on the specificity of the culturally embedded reference scheme of Western tonal music as compared to music of non-Western people. A key influence at the laboratory was German philosopher and experimental psychologist Carl Stumpf, with whom Myers kept close professional ties.[42] Stumpf's pioneering work in tone psychology and the ethnological study of so-called "primitive music" was well assimilated into Myers's own scientific thinking and research on these subjects.

Wittgenstein's initiation into Myers's laboratory occurred in the aftermath of a fierce debate in the 1890s in experimental psychology between Carl Stumpf and Wilhelm Wundt concerning the role of musical skills and expertise in the laboratory study of tone differentiation.[43] For Stumpf, sound sensation (pertaining to music) was bound up with musical training and musical aesthetics. Musical expertise was rendered as a criterion for credibility, and considered also to be a scientific skill, connoting superior ability to experience sound. By contrast, Wundt found little need for his subjects to maintain a superior ability to recognize Western musical intervals. He privileged large aggregates of data and statistical analysis over the subjective testimony of a few well-trained observers.[44] The fact that Myers's laboratory reverently sided with Stumpf's paradigm is most important for our present concern. Siding with Stumpf meant that the difference between musical individuals and nonmusical individuals was taken to be informative and important for grasping what is "musical" about music.

Under Stumpf's influence, the understanding of musicality at Myers's laboratory was twofold. First, musicality is aspectual in the sense that it is evinced by the ability of musical subjects to characterize what they hear musically. For nonmusical people, the particular mode of characterization, which is the reference scheme of Western tonal music, is inaccessible or obfuscated. Second, such characterizing requires an emphasis on specific techniques that inhere in our varied lived, culturally embedded, and embodied realities of musical intelligibility.

The idea of characterization as the hallmark of musicality is related to Stumpf's celebrated notion of "tonal fusion" (*Tonverschmelzung*) that became prevalent in Myers's laboratory.[45] According to Stumpf (1883), fusion is a tendency of the

---

[42] Stumpf's philosophical work was also well-known in Cambridge, and he was read with keen interest by the likes of McTaggart and G. E. Moore, with whom the young Wittgenstein was closely associated. Wittgenstein may even have read some of Stumpf's philosophical writings. See Potter (2008, 105–106).

[43] See Hui (2013), Chapter 5.

[44] Wittgenstein's rejection of this kind of experimental approach to matters concerning aesthetics is most apparent in his 1938 lectures on aesthetics. See LC, III:1–11.

[45] Myers often used Stumpf's notion of "tonal fusion," and the work of C. W. Valentine (1962), Myers's collaborator at the laboratory at the time, is also replete with references to Stumpf's ideas and writings. It is quite likely that Wittgenstein encountered Stumpf's notion of "tonal

subject's judgments to remain in a state of sensation (*Empfindung*), which precedes the subject's access to, and her ability to implement, the musical reference scheme and so to characterize what she hears musically, which is the state of "analysis." Stumpf suggested that the greater the tendency of sounds to fuse, the greater the consonance. Hence, while experiencing two tones as consonant is naturally given in sensation, common to nonmusical and musically skilled subjects alike, experiencing two tones as dissonant is unique to musical subjects, who can perceptually advance beyond the state of sensation into the state of analysis.

According to Kursell (2019), Stumpf realized that what nonmusical subjects lacked was not the ability to discriminate a physically measurable difference in frequency, but a mental scheme to which musically versatile listeners referred any such distances, thereby turning them into intervals and thus into musically relevant distances. Since musical subjects always apply this reference scheme, a value on the parameter of pitch would not simply be considered a distance, but referred to points of orientation, i.e., to the closest interval. Stumpf (1883, 149) described this reference scheme metaphorically as having "clear, fixed signposts of acoustic geodesy within musical contexts." Nonmusical subjects have no access to such musical cartography. They cannot characterize what they hear musically. They simply get lost in the territory.

Yet such "signposts of acoustic geodesy," the elements of the relevant musical cartography, if you will, are fixed only by virtue of culturally contracted ways of hearing, through close dialogue with musical environments, local traditions, and individual habits. Such ways of hearing are embedded in the common practice of music and the various aspects of the life of a culture which sustains it, and they are inscribed in particular notations for particular musical languages. This was a profound lesson, which both Stumpf and Myers learned as pioneers in the ethnological study of non-Western music. The understanding that a given "musical cartography" is always the product of specific musical training and circumstances brought into question the innateness of the Western tonal system. Moreover, the encounter with the music of non-Western people also gave rise to an acute awareness on the part of the researcher of his own mental presets in hearing the music and the way in which these presets are inscribed into the common practice notational system. The acquiring and accommodating of musical presets different from ours are uncannily conditioned upon an attempt to recapture the experience of the nonmusical person. One needs to learn to hear anew.

---

fusion" at least indirectly by consulting Myers's *Text-Book of Experimental Psychology, with Laboratory Exercises.*

I maintain (Guter 2024) that these early lessons from Stumpf about musicality, which Wittgenstein learned at Myers's laboratory, namely, the significance of the ability to characterize and the importance of the specific ways we characterize, including the choices and the risks that we take in characterizing, remained fundamental to Wittgenstein's thinking about, and through music as he forged ahead with fully developing the analogy between the articulation of genuinely musical characteristics and meaningful characteristics of thought in language. The distinction between the musical and the unmusical remained important for Wittgenstein, giving rise throughout his writings to the two parallel axes, which I discussed in the previous section – the language-as-music axis and the music reproduction mechanisms axis. They culminate in the comparison in the *Philosophical Investigations* between understanding a musical theme and understanding a sentence in language and in his consideration of aspect-blindness, including the lack of ability to experience the meaning of words, which he compared to lacking a musical ear.[46] This matter is complemented by Wittgenstein's continued interest, following lessons from Stumpf's and Myers's comparative study of the music of non-Western peoples, in the difficulty involved in acquiring and accommodating the "alternative presets," so to speak, for understanding church (or ancient) modes, which existed before the common-practice era in Western music.[47] Indeed, the most enduring, and by far the deepest theme, which Wittgenstein carried over from Stumpf is encapsulated in the quote from Goethe's *Faust*, which dawned upon both thinkers: "In the beginning was the deed."[48] Upon the anthropological turn, which marked Wittgenstein's middle period, that theme propelled him away from the initial orbit of the *Tractatus*.

2.3 Paring Down the Master Simile

Against this backdrop of Wittgenstein's interests and philosophical develop-ment, the distinct austerity and meagerness of Wittgenstein's treatment of music in the *Tractatus* draws one's attention. One may very well wonder what Wittgenstein's view of music could have been at the time of the *Tractatus*.[49]

---

[46] I return to these topics in Section 4.

[47] Wittgenstein first mentioned the problem of understanding a church mode in 1930 in the context of discussing the issue of noticing an aspect, then again in 1933 in the context of discussing his experiments at Myers's laboratory, and the issue was evoked lastly in *Philosophical Investigations* in the context of the language-as-music simile, and in other later writings. See PR, 281 §224; WLM, 9:41; PI, 152 §535; RPPI, 118 §639. See also my (Guter 2020) analysis of Wittgenstein's discussion in WLM, 9:41.

[48] Cf. Stumpf (2012), 68; OC §402; CV, 36 [31].

[49] Some (Ahonen 2005; Appelqvist 2023; Szabados 2014) argue that the early Wittgenstein was a musical formalist à la Eduard Hanslick, whose roots go deep into Kantian philosophy. I return to this suggestion in the next section and also in Section 4.2. Others (Eggers 2014; Wright 2007)

I maintain (Guter 2024) that Wittgenstein has not changed his original view on music, but that the mounting logical pressure of his *Tractatus* framework resulted in the elision of musicality from that particular work at that particular period in his philosophical evolution. What has been elided rebounded in the aftermath of the *Tractatus* in the early 1930s. Thus, my reading of music in the *Tractatus* is deflationary in a sense not unlike Wittgenstein's famous remark to Ludwig von Ficker about the "unwritten part" of the *Tractatus* (minus the transcendental baggage). From the perspective of the later Wittgenstein, what he has suppressed regarding music was more important.

The only remark on music from Wittgenstein's *Notebooks 1914–1916* that made the cut to the published version of the *Tractatus* was the one in which Wittgenstein presented for the first time the master simile of language-as-music in an explicit analogy between "a word mixture" and "a tone mixture" (NB, 41).[50] Yet importantly, the master simile was eventually introduced into the *Tractatus* (TLP, 3.141) in a peculiarly truncated, tamed down form. The original language-as-music simile as suggested in the *Notebooks* was bound to be challenged and ultimately stultified within the emerging *Tractatus* framework. Wittgenstein's grappling with the original simile is evident in his textual alterations and editing decisions during the complex transition from the early remarks in the *Notebooks* to the *Prototractatus* and then to the ultimate bilingual publication of the *Tractatus* in 1922.[51]

In the *Notebooks*, Wittgenstein introduced the master simile in two juxtaposing entries, written a week apart. The first concerned a sentence in language, then came the afterthought concerning a melody.

> The sentence is not a word mixture (NB, 41 [5.4.15]).[52]
> Nor is a melody a tone mixture, as all unmusical people think.
> (NB, 41 [11.4.15])[53]

A sentence in language is compared to a melody in the sense of not being a mixture of the respective sort. Thinking of a melody in terms of a "tone mixture" (*Tongesmisch*) is typical, Wittgenstein adds, of unmusical (*unmusikalisch*)

---

argue that Wittgenstein should be seen as sharing some sort of allegiance with composer Arnold Schoenberg's embarking on a new musical language in the spirit of logical positivism. See my extensive rebuttal of this suggestion in Guter (2011).

[50] The other significant remark on music in the *Tractatus* is the gramophone analogy (TLP, 4.014–4.0141), which I discuss in the next section. However, the gramophone analogy did not originate in the early *Notebooks*, and its substantial second part was redacted from the original 1921 publication.

[51] See my detailed analysis of this textual evolution in Guter (2024).

[52] I modified the translation. Wittgenstein himself opted for the word "mixture" (see LO, 34).

[53] I modified the translation. The German term *Tongemisch* is highly unusual in this context. This oddity is important, I maintain, and ought to be preserved in English.

people. Two things immediately draw one's attention in this remark: we require a proper understanding of the very idea of "tone mixture" (a rather strange coinage, both in the original German and in English), which also takes into account Wittgenstein's peculiar reference to "unmusical people." Acknowledging Wittgenstein's exposure to Stumpf's ideas on musicality at Myers's laboratory allows us to frame this version of the simile aright, hence, to see what happened to it along the way to its final version in the *Tractatus*, and also why.

Stumpf afforded Wittgenstein with a concrete understanding of the connection between being unmusical and failing in tone judgment. Reacting directly to the degree of tonal fusion, nonmusical people practically get lost in the territory of music. They have no clear, fixed signposts of acoustic geodesy within musical contexts, Stumpf says. Hence, their judgment of tones is flawed, which impairs their ability to participate in musical practices. It stands to reason that Wittgenstein opted for the unusual term "tone mixture" (*Tongemisch*) in relation to Stumpf's notion of "tonal fusion" (*Tonverschmelzung*). It is in this sense that a melody can be coherently said to be a *Tongemisch* for unmusical people, who can still recognize the contour of a melody as such and may even attempt to whistle it (albeit not quite successfully).[54] As a false judgment of tones the "tone mixture" is due to tonal fusion unchecked by the "musical" features of music: primarily, a failure to *characterize* tone distance as intervals, that is, as musically relevant distances. Since truth or falsity in the judgment of tones hinges upon the individuation of which among the variety of possible ways of hearing is asserted on a given occasion, rendering a melody as "tone mixture" pertains to a failure in the ineliminable exercise of mutual tuning-in relationships.

In this sense, Wittgenstein's original analogy between "tone mixture" and "word mixture" turns out too philosophically robust and potent vis-à-vis the *Tractatus* framework. It also introduces an anomaly, since Wittgenstein does not tell us what the analog in the realm of language for being unmusical would be. Unmusical people (in Stumpf's sense) are what the later Wittgenstein would call "aspect-blind." They have no access to the musical cartography, which is the acquired, culturally embedded, and embodied presets of what Stumpf called "music consciousness." And so, they cannot characterize what they hear musically, in a living way. Yet in the realm of language the analog of meaning-blindness far exceeds the framework of the *Tractatus*. It revolves on all those arbitrary correlations between signs and objects, which the author of the *Tractatus* decidedly brushes aside.

---

[54] It is unlikely that Wittgenstein would have confused between unmusical individuals and individuals who are afflicted by congenital amusia, hence are literally tone- or tune-deaf.

If Wittgenstein took his initial lead from Stumpf concerning unmusical people, then we have to say that while sentences and melodies are both not mixtures of their respective elements, it is nonetheless not quite in the same sense, *pace* the author of the *Tractatus*. In the *Tractatus*, saying that a sentence is not a word mixture amounts to saying that "the sentence is articulate" (TLP, 3.141). The idea that a sentence is articulate means that it has structure: a sentence is a determinate combination of elements.[55] Of course, the melody is also articulate. If a melody did not inhere in a structure from the start, that is, if its constituent parts are supposed to be mere pitch values, then understanding a melody would have amounted to being able to discriminate a physically measurable difference in frequency. Wittgenstein clearly set himself to reject such a view when thinking in terms of articulate pictures.

Yet, the idea of a melody as a structure remains very thin (i.e., aptly logical) in the sense that it does not (and not supposed to) tell us anything about any particular capacities of any particular musical language. Importantly, the philosophical lesson from Stumpf and Myers was that the answer to the question what the musical features of music are requires an emphasis on the ineliminable importance of the culturally situated wherewithal for a myriad of enormously complex techniques of characterizing that we employ to communicate musically. Within the *Tractatus* framework, a melody can be said to be a structure only if one takes for granted that all those arbitrary correlations have already been taken care of and have been fixed. This is where we can observe the almost inevitable elision in the *Tractatus* of musicality understood (via Stumpf and Myers) as inhering precisely in the arbitrariness of such correlations.

In the *Tractatus*, the importance of internal projective relations far exceeds that of arbitrariness in language. According to Floyd (2018a, 373–374),

> the *Tractatus* aimed to assure, with one grand gesture, that the possibility of all possibilities, of all possible parametrizations, *must* work out, inscribed in the schematic structure of the general form of proposition. [. . .] The *Tractatus* idea is that what belongs to logic as such shows forth anyway, regardless of what we do in concocting particular forms of charactery and characterization.

Eliding musicality accords with Wittgenstein's philosophical incentive in the *Tractatus* to belittle the specific techniques of characterization involved in symbolizations and representations of all kinds.

Wittgenstein's repeating alterations of the *Notebooks* version of the master simile attest to his attempt to tame it down philosophically, so it would fit the needs of the *Tractatus*. This called first and foremost for the suppression of the underlying Stumpfian distinction between musical and unmusical people, and

---

[55] Cf. LO, 34.

its apposite analog in the realm of language. Indeed in the transition from the *Notebooks* version to its counterpart in the *Prototractatus* (PT, 3.1602–3), the reference to unmusical people has been conspicuously dropped together with the Stumpfian sounding term "tone mixture," which is replaced by the more colloquial phrase "a mixture of tones," thereby rhetorically shifting the focus away from tone judgment to the consideration of structure per se. Wittgenstein also replaced the reference to a melody with a reference to a musical theme. This also makes sense, if Wittgenstein wanted to push the envelope on the similarity between language and music in terms of sentential structure, since, musically speaking, a musical theme is patently also a (musical) sentence, whereas a melody is not (unless it is used as a musical theme in a composition).

Thus, we find in the *Tractatus* (TLP, 3.141) the final version of the master simile, which elides musicality quite straightforwardly:

> The sentence is not a word mixture. – (Just as the musical theme is not a mixture of tones.)
> The sentence is articulate.[56]

The highly potent directionality of the language-as-music simile has in fact been pared down to the point of mere symmetry to accommodate Wittgenstein's idea of logical structure in the *Tractatus*.

2.4 The Gramophone Analogy

Wittgenstein's preemptive move to pare down the language-as-music simile sets the stage for his gramophone analogy (TLP, 4.014–4.0141), which, as I argued in Section 1.2, strikingly introduces in his discussion of music an allusion to a mechanical device which would consistently epitomize the idea of unmusicality throughout his entire oeuvre.

The analogy is an amalgamation of two distinct parts. The first part (TLP, 4.014) already appeared in the *Prototractatus* (PT, 4.01141–4.011411). Wittgenstein presents a comparison between four things: the musical score, the musical thought, the music (problematically referred to as sound-waves), and the gramophone record. The notion of structure features prominently as the analogy serves to exemplify Wittgenstein's picture theory: "To all of them the logical structure is common" (TLP, 4.014). The analogy is supposed to elucidate

---

[56] I modified the translation. A more literal translation of *Wörtergemisch* serves as a foil for Wittgenstein's final rephrasing of the musical analog. For the kind of close tracking of Wittgenstein's textual modifications, which is called for here, I prefer Ogden's overly literal translation, which has been approved by Wittgenstein, over the more eloquent one by Pears and McGuinness.

Wittgenstein's idea that language stands in an internal relation of depicting to the world. Once again, it is instructive to pay close attention to Wittgenstein's editing decisions and his recasting of the text. In the *Prototractatus* the gramophone analogy is preceded by the claim that "The possibility of all similes, of all the imagery of our language, rests on the logic of representation," whereas in the *Tractatus* the order is reversed (PT, 4.0101; cf. TLP, 4.015). According to Floyd (2018a), the idea here is that what belongs to logic as such shows forth anyway, regardless of what we do in concocting particular forms of charactery and characterization. This colors the gramophone analogy; in effect, whatever Wittgenstein was trying to spell out by means of the gramophone analogy has already been predisposed by this view of logic.

Wittgenstein's emphasis on structure prompted a construal of his view of music at the time of the *Tractatus* as musical formalism, understood along lines attributed to the work of Hanslick (2018) as the inseparability of form and content in music.[57] Hanslick famously contended that the content of music consists entirely of "sonically moved forms" (*tönend bewegte Formen*). Wittgenstein's ultimately pared down version of the language-as-music simile (TLP, 3.141) seems to concur with this: the musical theme is played and heard as being articulate. Wittgenstein's explicit use of the term "musical thought" (*musikalische Gedanke*) in the gramophone analogy may also hint at Hanslick, but this cannot be firmly confirmed.[58] As a technical term, "musical thought" was featured extensively in music theory treatises at least since Johann Quantz in the eighteenth century, and it commonly designated a melody or a theme. Wittgenstein's use of the term as it has been commonly understood may simply reiterate what he already claimed in the *Tractatus* version of the master simile. Thus, we can replace the term "musical thought" in the gramophone analogy with the term "musical theme" at no cost. The comparison would be between a musical theme, the appropriate sound-waves, the score, and the gramophone record – "To all of them the logical structure is common." Hanslick (2018, 43–44) related the term "musical thought" to the idea of musical logic, which he understood as the sophisticated unfolding of the development of a theme. The point here, once again, concerns articulation. Hence, the similarity to Hanslick may be purely coincidental.

Yet, furthermore, my construction of the text suggests that musical forms can be said to be "sonically moved" only if we grant that all the arbitrary correlations at the bottom of our culturally contracted reference scheme of Western

---

[57] See Ahonen (2005), Appelqvist (2023), and Szabados (2014).

[58] Soulez (2006) insists that this is actually Schoenberg's concept. However, this most certainly cannot be the case since Schoenberg only started to work out his own concept of the *musikalische Gedanke* in his manuscripts in 1923, two years after the publication of the *Tractatus*.

tonal music have already been fixed, as if what Stumpf called "signposts of acoustic geodesy within musical contexts" consisted in absolute simplicity, foreclosing indeterminacy and arbitrariness. I agree with Floyd (2018a) that, from the point of view of the later Wittgenstein, such belittling of the specific techniques of characterization involved in symbolizations and representations of all kinds can be seen as a deep lacuna at the heart of the *Tractatus*. Thus, I contend (Guter 2024) that what may look like musical formalism in the *Tractatus* can be seen as the corona that encircles the eclipse of the philosophical significance of musicality at that stage in the evolution of Wittgenstein's thinking.

The second part of the analogy (TLP, 4.0141) intensifies that eclipse. This segment, known as "Supplement no. 72," was a very late addition to the final form of the *Tractatus*. This was one of about a hundred scraps, which Wittgenstein was unsure whether to incorporate into his work or not, and he decided (quite reluctantly) to add it to the original statement of the gramophone analogy upon the request of C. K. Ogden during the proofing stage of the *Tractatus* in 1922.[59] This late addition draws out the blatantly mechanical, unmusical aspect of the gramophone analogy, first and foremost by dropping the notion of "musical thought" out of consideration quite inexplicably. We remain with the music (now referred to as "the symphony"), the score, and the gramophone record, and the discussion revolves on the idea of deriving one from another by means of a law of projection. As a technology, the gramophone has a clear advantage for Wittgenstein's purpose in effacing itself in the idealizing of "the symphony" as pure structure. Yet this self-effacement also masks an inherent mishap for the portrayal of isomorphism. As Kittler (1999, 35) pointed out, "time axis reversal, which the phonograph makes possible, allows ears to hear the unheard-of: the steep attack of instrumental sounds or spoken syllables moves to the end, while the much longer decay moves to the front." The problem is that there is no straightforwardly meaningful equivalent for such mechanical reversal of structure either in the domain of the score or in the domain of the music-as-heard, at least within the reasonable confines of common-practice era music.

The supplemented part of the gramophone analogy only aggravates this difficulty. Wittgenstein relies on inter-translatability – rendering the symphony, the score, and the gramophone record as mutually translatable languages – to substantiate his notion of isomorphism. Yet the idea of isomorphism glosses over profound asymmetries between the various tasks involved in each inter-mediary step of the inter-translation as posited in the gramophone analogy. Comparing the process of derivation involved in the human activities of writing

---

[59] See LO, 26; 39–40; 46.

or playing music to the mechanistic inscription or derivation of sound via the groove in a gramophone readily evokes his later critical consideration of reading machines; therein lies the straightforward connection between the gramophone analogy and Wittgenstein's later allusions to the pianola, as I argued in the previous section.[60] Wittgenstein's "musician" in the gramophone analogy is as fictitious as the human reading machine in *Philosophical Investigations* (PI §156; cf. PG, 191), who can produce the right sounds on seeing the written signs, whether or not he understands those signs; only the former is said to be capable also of the reverse feat, namely, producing the right written signs on hearing the sounds, by virtue of the same mechanism.

From the perspective of a real practicing musician, one who makes music with understanding, this is quite wrongheaded. The purported isomorphism is inevitably cluttered and unevenly parsed by the enormously complicated conventions and activities on which musical understanding depends. Neither performing a symphony from a score nor deriving a score from a performance of a symphony allows for mechanical reversibility as in recording and playback. In both cases, intermediate steps depend on human agency, but the required musical tasks, skills, and sensitivities are profoundly different. Performing a symphony from a score calls for interpretation, phrasing, and characterizing of a situated performance of the symphony, expressing specific choices in real time by the performers in the given acoustic space. Identical renditions are impossible (or, at least, unimportant); only new realizations matter. This is a common practice, familiar to many – performers and audience alike.

However, deriving the musical score from a given performance of a symphony is a highly specific, even rare, feat. It calls for outstanding dictation skills, which are not so common even among professional musicians. The process is prone to many inaccuracies and unforeseeable anomalies due to built-in limitations of the notational system, different possible ways of notating certain musical elements (even concerning the same pitch, as in the case of enharmonic spelling), specific difficulties concerning choral dictations, and diversities due to agogic stress and phrasing in the actual performance. Most importantly, deriving a score from performance is a highly specialized task that normally serves a particularly professional purpose: practicing, sketching, capturing an aspect of the music for future reference, and so forth.

The gramophone analogy is sustained by glossing over the very notion of human agency pertaining to music-making, that is, by suppressing the very fact, undeniably known to Wittgenstein only too well, that music is commonly bestowed upon us by virtue of the mutual tuning-in relationships between

---

[60] See Section 1.2.

musically trained individuals in performance. This can be observed in two corollaries to the gramophone analogy, which Sterrett (2005) points out. The first concerns the nature of the score as a picture of the music. From the standpoint of logical structure, the features of the symphony must be only those features of the symphony that are used in applying the rule by which the score is obtained from the symphony. The isomorphism is based upon just those features of the symphony that can be projected into the score. Hence only what is relevant to the mode of depiction belongs to the logical structure shared by the depiction and the depicted. This would mean that the peculiarities of an individual performance, unless they are captured in both the musical score and the gramophone lines, are not considered part of the logical structure of the symphony performance. Since any individual performance is patently underdetermined by the score – in common practice era music to various degrees, and even more so in ancient and contemporary notation (e.g., graphic notation) – this comes down to a meagre image of music in terms of pure inter-translatability.[61]

The second corollary concerns the nature of musical notation. According to the gramophone analogy, whatever musical notation is in use dictates what is and is not included in the logical structure of the symphony. This has an interesting consequence: the logical structure of the symphony is not something independent of language and absolute but is relative to the musical notation used to depict it. Yet, as I argued earlier in this section, a crucial lesson from Stumpf's and Myers's comparative study of non-Western music was that the built-in limitations of the musical notation that we use embody our open-ended culturally contracted mental presets that allow for music to be appreciated musically. Wittgenstein remained silent on this matter due to the need in the *Tractatus* framework to reflect on the idea of a common logical form. Eliding musicality (including the distinction between musical and unmusical people) among all other deep-seated complex human competencies, which extend to the very capability of language itself (see TLP, 4.002), allows for a neat presentation of the picture theory by drawing out the specter of mechanical inscription and derivation within music.

3 The Middle Period: Reorienting Depth

3.1 Three Trajectories

Wittgenstein's transitional middle period is characterized by an abundance of remarks on music of all sorts, and by the thriving of the language-as-music

---

[61] It is noteworthy that upon reconsidering his picture theory in a lecture on March 13, 1933 (WLM, 8: 53), Wittgenstein was quick to bring up the case of the score as a picture of the music: "First note: (what I hadn't then noticed) that idea of 'picture' is vague: e.g. score is 'picture' of music."

simile now unbound by the *Tractatus* framework. Remarks from this period also solidified the axis of Wittgenstein's consistent allusions to mechanical means of musical reproduction, which I discussed in Section 1,[62] when considering human reading machines and human playing machines as a foil to highlighting what I dub "mutual tuning-in relationships."

The passage from Wittgenstein's 1930 letter to Koder, which opened Section 1, shows that musical thinking afforded Wittgenstein with a pioneering glimpse of what Floyd (2016, 2017) calls the "fluidity of simplicity." Wittgenstein's 1933 (WLM, 9:40–42) recounting his 1912–1913 experiments on rhythm, which I discussed in Section 2, show that already before the *Tractauts*, his thinking about, and through music allowed him to entertain the possibility that "simples" are open-ended, humanly textured, a matter of ongoing conversation, rather than fixed and absolute. By the years 1936–1937, on completely independent grounds, as Floyd (2016) shows, Wittgenstein was able to fully embrace the radical idea, pioneered already in 1930 in the privacy of his letter to Koder, that simplicity is fluid. Fluidity is shown in that we always must start somewhere, we always take something to be simple, evident, unproblematic, be it a passage in the score or one's initial tendency to realize it in a certain way, following certain rules. Yet new "voices" turn up and others slip away, as Wittgenstein wrote to Koder, and such partial procedures, as in phrasing a passage in the score, are sometimes partially defined, dropped, detached, refashioned, amalgamated, reoriented, reframed, and revisited. For Wittgenstein this is true not only for music making in the sense of performance, but also for music making in the sense of composing, and by extension to musical tradition as a whole. The rules of harmony (*Harmonielehre*) are given to us as such because they "are here and are part of our entire life" (MS157a, 24–26), and every composer changed the rules, even ever so slightly (LC, I:16). The way music evolves is not just the background for the composer's search, it is also an ongoing, open-ended encounter with the search itself, with our inherited quest for culture.

Wittgenstein's middle-period remarks on music reveal his progression toward the fluidity of simplicity as an interweaving of three distinct trajectories: (a) the emergence of the "anthropological view"; (b) the revolt against cultural decline; and (c) the relation of music to concepts of the inner. I discuss them below in this order. These themes feature prominently in Wittgenstein's texts and lectures from the 1930s, as musical examples are used to tease out the conversational, open-ended nature of attending to aesthetic puzzles, the

---

[62] See Section 1.2. To that one may also add Wittgenstein's (RFM I §123ff) discussion of human calculators in his philosophy of mathematics.

prominence of comparisons and characterizing, and the reliance of all that on shape-shifting resemblances that unify our way of life.

Stern (1991) usefully describes the trajectory of the emergence of Wittgenstein's anthropological view as a progression from logical atomism (the doctrine that all meaningful discourse can be analyzed into logically independent elementary propositions) to logical holism (the thesis that analysis leads to systems of logically related propositions and that language is a formal system of rules), and from logical holism to practical holism (the view that our coping with things and people in, and through language can only be meaningful in specific contexts and against the background of shared practices). The anthropological view, which became a staple of Wittgenstein's methodology in his later philosophy, from the early 1936 version of *Philosophical Investigations* onward, brought into prominence the idea that a full understanding of the role of signs in a language requires looking at how signs relate to the form of life of which they are part. The turning point was ultimately due to the stimulus of economist Piero Sraffa's criticism on Wittgenstein's ideas in the *Big Typescript* (TS 213), which Wittgenstein assembled between the years 1932–1933.[63] Sraffa's criticism prompted Wittgenstein's to reconsider the philosophical import of gestures, that is, signs, which (when taken in isolation) we could not give a grammar. Wittgenstein realized that in the case of gestures – music-making affords countless examples of different kinds, as Wittgenstein himself observed – we have to look at the environment, the surroundings, where the language functions, that is, the form of life.

Importantly, already in the *Tractatus* Wittgenstein allowed for a glimpse of the relevance of an open-ended notion of human life when he wrote (TLP, 4.002) that "colloquial language is a part of the human organism and is no less complicated than it. [...] The silent adjustments to understand colloquial language are enormously complicated." As Tejedor (2015) noted, this is a precursor to Wittgenstein's later notion of a form of life. The facts relevant to human life include the facts about our physical environment, about our human biology and about our human psychology, which play out in our differently enculturated forms of life. The acknowledgment of the enormous complexity pertaining to the facts of human life is there in the *Tractatus* for Wittgenstein to lean on, but the matter itself remains underdeveloped until the anthropological turn in Wittgenstein's middle period, which enabled him to bring in a more articulate sense of the arbitrary.

Within the framework of the *Tractatus*, musicality, in the sense that he learned at Myers's laboratory, ended up being bracketed as belonging to those

---

[63] See Engelmann (2013).

enormously complicated "silent adjustments to understand colloquial language." The elision of musicality in the *Tractatus* mirrors something that Wittgenstein later came see as a general difficulty with the *Tractatus* that was not so clear to him at the time when he wrote it: the idea that "colloquial language is a part of the human organism and is no less complicated than it" remained an underdeveloped aspect of his early philosophy. If Wittgenstein struggled with these ideas and could not quite get settled with them, kept them out of the *Tractatus*, and only came back to them later, then it is fair to say, I maintain, that it is because in the *Tractatus*, having suppressed the importance of the specific ways we characterize, Wittgenstein was left without any way to develop the master simile of language-as-music. Once the anthropological turn sets in, thinking about music and musicality became available to Wittgenstein as an excellent point of entry for that more dynamic field of concepts.

The second trajectory – the revolt against cultural decline – interlinks with the first trajectory and with the third. Wittgenstein's anthropological turn was prefigured and prepped by his early exposure to Stumpf's ideas and methodologies, but also by reading Oswald Spengler's *Decline of the West* in May of 1930. He noted in his diary (MT, 25): "Reading Spengler Decline etc. & in spite of many irresponsibilities in the particulars, find many real, significant thoughts. Much, perhaps most of it, is completely in touch with what I have often thought myself." Spengler's ideas about the morphological study of cultures propelled (albeit by way of criticism) Wittgenstein's growing fascination with the possibility of philosophizing by means of making illuminating comparisons, and as Wittgenstein's lectures in Cambridge in the 1930s make evident, this exerted a particular influence on his conception of aesthetics.

Furthermore, according to Von Wright (1982, 118), under the influence of Spengler,

> Wittgenstein [...] thought that the problems with which he was struggling were somehow connected with "the way people live," that is, with features of our culture or civilization to which he and his pupils belonged. [...] His way of doing philosophy was not an attempt to tell us what philosophy, once and for all, *is* but expressed what for him, in the setting of the times, it had to be.

In the passage to the time of civilization, the time without culture, Wittgenstein believed, we lose a community, an inheritance, a shared sense of life, and natural (as opposed to artificial) forms of interaction and expression.[64] He expressed his trepidations about philosophizing amid cultural decline quite openly to his

---

[64] See Wittgenstein's sketch for a forward to *Philosophical Remarks*, written around the same time (CV, 8–9 [6–7]).

students in Cambridge at the time. "Philosophy is reduced to a matter of skill," he said in his opening lecture for Michaelmas Term in 1930 (WLM, 5:2).

> This doesn't mean that progress has occurred; but that style of thinking has changed = nimbus of philosophy has been lost. [. . .] The moment a method is found, one way of expressing personality is lost. And there's no reason to be sorry for this. General tendency of this age is to take away possibilities of expression: which is characteristic of age without a culture.

Yet, according to Cavell (1996), far beyond dwelling in mere lamentation for all the cultural manifestations prescribed by the form of progress in a time without culture – compulsive overstructuring and obfuscation, and with it, a fragmentation into calculable objects that leaves no room for the expression of personality ("none for nimbus") – Wittgenstein's own philosophical course from that point onward to *Philosophical Investigations*, including the emergence of his mature interlocutory style of writing, became a preoccupation with the very features of civilization that Spengler thought of as typical of cultural decline, carrying out his intention to combat the conditions of cultural decline as they manifest themselves in the misuses of language that characterize the errant thoughts of philosophers.

Around the same time, Wittgenstein also became acquainted to some extent with the music theory of Heinrich Schenker through conversations with musicologist Felix Salzer (Wittgenstein's nephew), who studied with Schenker in Vienna from 1931 until the latter's death in 1935.[65] The conversations with Salzer, in which Wittgenstein was mostly interested in his own ideas on Schenker's theory, began in 1926 and continued into the early 1930s during summers at the *Hochreit*, the Wittgenstein family country estate.[66] Schenker, who shared a similar worldview with Spengler,[67] offered a formidable theory of musical decline, which derives from his grand idea that all works of music (in particular all masterworks) are essentially extended commentaries on the major triad. The most background formation from which any composition can be directly derived is the triad in motion, as represented in Schenker's idea of *Ursatz*. This fundamental structure is famously shown in the formations of Schenker's bass arpeggiation of tonic-dominant-tonic (I-V-I). In Schenkerian analysis, the quality of a musical work depends on whether it has the type of expansion ("middleground" layers) that could connect its surface or "foreground" to a constant "background" and, ultimately, to the *Ursatz*. Any musical work that digresses from common practice harmony (hence failing to

---

[65] Salzer immigrated to the United States in 1939 and became a world-renowned champion of Schenker's ideas and analytic method.
[66] See Guter (2015).   [67] See Almén (1996).

demonstrate the kind of hierarchy, which Schenkerian analysis seeks out) is patently rejected by Schenker as unsuccessful, superficial, or altogether music-ally nonsensical, depending on the severity of the digression. Schenker's theory gave him concrete means by which to diagnose the disintegration of musical culture on all fronts. Irreverence to the laws of tonal effect, among performers and composers alike, reflected, so he believed, a loss of musical instinct for the inner complexities of the masterworks of Western music, which in turn hindered the musician's almost sacred mission to provide access to the world of human experience contained in such masterworks.[68]

In the context of Wittgenstein's anthropological turn, his contention that Schenker's theory needs to be "boiled down" – as Salzer reported to Brian McGuinness (Guter 2015) – can be readily understood as reflecting Wittgenstein's view, noted above, that the rules of harmony are given to us as such because they "are here and are part of our entire life" (MS 157a, 24–26). In this sense, Schenker's terms need to be brought back from their metaphysical to their everyday use (cf. PI §116). Furthermore, for Wittgenstein (BT, 204),[69] Schenker's theoretical adherence to the *Ursatz* exemplifies the same problem, which he detected in Spengler's sorting of cultural epochs into families, ascrib-ing properties, which only the prototype or paradigm (*Urbild*) possesses, to the object that is viewed in its light.

Wittgenstein's point was that the conceptual relations within the prototype, relations which can be expressed as grammatical or conceptual necessities, need to characterize the whole discussion, and determine its form; however, they do not and cannot shape the phenomena that are being discussed. "The only way namely for us to avoid prejudice – or vacuity in our claims," Wittgenstein (CV, 30 [26]) wrote, "is to posit the ideal as what it is, namely as an object of comparison – a measuring rod as it were – within our way of looking at things, & not as a preconception to which everything must con-form." Thus, from Wittgenstein's perspective, Schenker erred in his dogmatic use of the notion of *Ursatz*. Accepting the idea that all good works of music are exfoliations of a primal musical phenomenon does not entail that we are bound by a preconception to which everything must conform. Rather, it is a way of characterizing what one hears by means of setting actual works of music in surveyable order within our way of looking at things. As Wittgenstein (MS 153b, 60v–61r) noted, "considering the piece in Schenker's way" is only one

---

[68] See Snarrenberg (1997, 145–150).

[69] Wittgenstein added a handwritten comment "Schenker's way of looking at music" next to the passage, which introduces the concept of "family resemblance" by means of a critique of Spengler's principle of comparative morphology of cultural epochs. Cf. WLM, 9:33.

way, intertwined with many others, for showing that one hears with understanding.

The third trajectory – the relation of music to concepts of the inner – draws the longest arch in our story since it allows for reintroducing Wittgenstein historically as an intermediary figure of a unique stature in the passage from Romanticism to contemporary philosophy of music. The very idea that music relates to the inner, indeed to self-knowledge, appears in a clear voice at the end of the passage on music from Wittgenstein's letter to Koder: "Listen carefully and follow what [the inner voices] say to you, and you will see, you will then hear more and more distinctly, and you will know more and more about yourself" (LK, 38). Music making, the activity of phrasing and characterizing, is soul-searching in the sense of lending oneself to an acquaintance with possibilities of human expression.

Wittgenstein's position in the letter brings into the fore a distinctive facet of Romanticism, which Charles Taylor (1996) dubbed "the expressivist turn": the idea that music enshrines an inexhaustible inner domain whose contents are not reducible, not collectible, not calculable, hence could never be fully articulated. The most obvious influence on Wittgenstein concerning this exalted stature of music among the arts was Schopenhauer, whom Wittgenstein read early on and in 1931 even named him (together with Spengler, Sraffa and others) one of the thinkers whose line of thinking he seized on for his own work (CV, 16 [19]).

For Schopenhauer (1969), music has an exceptional place in the system of the arts. It is conceived to be radically different from, and superior to, all other arts in two correlated ways, metaphysical and aesthetic: it both expresses the will itself, intimating knowledge of ultimate reality in the most immediate, most vivid way, and speaks to us intensely about human reality, intimating knowledge of what Schopenhauer calls the "inner nature" of human emotion, or the "secret history" of the human will. Thus, the value of music lies, inter alia, in its unique kinship to the phenomenological dynamics of the human emotions, feelings, and moods, to the peculiar "feel" of their intensity, surge, waxing, and waning. This is a full-fledged philosophy of music in which the uncanny correspondence between the inner space of music and the inner space of the listening subject is sought out. Yet, for Schopenhauer, whatever music tells us with such intimacy and immediacy eludes comprehension by reason. Thus, what music means, what it is about, cannot be translated into other languages. It remains otherwise inexpressible and understanding what music is about amounts to gaining access to this otherwise inexpressible knowledge.

Another immediate source for such ideas about the inwardness of music were Spengler and Schenker. For Spengler (1939, vol. 1, 285–286), music reflects the Western soul, it is its prime symbol, best suited for its role as a medium for expressing the "Faustian" ideal of striving toward infinite space. The sacred role of the musician is to create with a few tones an image of inexhaustible content, a microcosm met for the ears of the "Faustian" man. Similarly, Schenker maintained that "in its linear progressions and comparable tonal events, music mirrors the human soul in all its metamorphoses and moods" (Cook 1989, 420). For Schenker, the deep structure, or background, that all great masterworks possess, lends them not only their coherence but also their cultural identity and value.

Wittgenstein's 1930 treatment of these themes in his letter to Koder already shows a substantial advancement over the Romantic take on the inwardness of music. In the context of Wittgenstein's growing emphasis on specific techniques of characterization and their open-ended embeddedness in a form of life, his tentative phrase "inner voices" in that letter can be best rendered in terms of the dynamic interplay of possibilities and necessities. Inwardness or depth is no longer a quasi-spatial notion, but rather logical. This means that the three trajectories, as they intertwine in Wittgenstein's progression toward the idea of the fluidity of simplicity, give rise to a reorientation of the notion of depth as pertaining to music and its importance in life.

3.2 Metaphors of Depth

Romantic German musical thought conceived musical depth as a spatial, yet nonvisual, metaphor. In the ordinary sense of "depth," we have a surface, which conceals what lies beneath it. If we dig into the surface, we may go deep, but then the depths revealed are no longer concealed. They become surface. By contrast, musical depth has been conceived as unsearchable depth, something that is not visually, namely, rationally accessible, hence remaining forever intractable, unfathomable, incalculable, ineffable, and untranslatable. Unlike linguistic and visual modes of expression, music is said to be capable of expanding one's sense of inner space beyond the limits prescribed by rationalism or by language. For that reason, music was exalted as the most profound of all arts.[70] This notion of musical depth reached full maturity and distinctiveness in the writings of philosophers, critics, music analysts, and composers around the mid-nineteenth century, and can be traced back to the writings of Johan Gottfried Herder, Wilhelm Heinrich Wackenroder, and E. T. A. Hoffmann. Watkins (2011) singles out E. T. A. Hoffman for suggesting the presence of a "vertical" dimension in music, perpendicular to its surface of temporal unfolding, thereby importing tensions endemic to Romantic metaphors of

---

[70] I return to the topic of musical profundity in Section 5.

depth – tensions between the knowable and the unknowable, and between rationality and irrationality – into the musical work.

This notion of musical depth is represented quite straightforwardly in a passage (CV, 11 [8–9]) that Wittgenstein penned sometime between 1931 and 1932. The passage exhibits the familiar contour of the Romantic view: the relation between a manifest surface and concealed content of infinite complexity, complete with an acute sense of the exalted status of music due to this concealment. It also suggests a direct influence by Spengler (1939, vol. 1, 285–286), who also referred to the musician as one who has the power to create an image of inexhaustible content with only a few tones, and from Schenker, whose *terminus technicus* "foreground" (*Vordergrund*) conspicuously crept into Wittgenstein's suggested variant in the text. Yet in the fleeting, shape-shifting context of Wittgenstein's middle period, we are left with a need to interpret the notion of "body" (*Körper*), which is said to have "all the infinity complexity that is suggested in the external forms of other arts." It is noteworthy that in this passage the term "content" (*Inhalt*) and the term "surface" are on a par. The "simple surface" *is* the "manifest content." This suggests that the infinite complexity of the musical gesture is not contained inside the musical work, but rather is embodied in the form of life of which it is a part, hence Wittgenstein's use of the word "body" (Körper). This renders the metaphoric orientation of depth very different from that of Romantic view.

To explicate Wittgenstein's shift in metaphors of depth, I avail myself of Lakoff and Johnson's (1980, 100–105) distinction between "container" metaphors of depth and "journey" metaphors of depth. Both types of metaphor define content in relation to surface, albeit in different ways. Containers define a limited space with a bounding surface, a center, and a periphery, as they hold a substance, which may vary in amount, and which may have a core located in the center. For the "container" metaphor, the content is inside the container, whose boundaries are defined by its surface. E. T. A. Hofmann's view epitomizes the "container" type, complete with a notion of the autonomous "thingness" of works of music *qua* containers of unfathomable depth. This conceptualization of vertical probing, a being launched from the variable surface of temporally unfolding sound structures into inexhaustible, inexplicable interiority, which is both our own innermost and the world's, reached saturation in the writings of Schopenhauer (1969, 264), for whom "the inexpressible depth of all music, by virtue of which it floats past us as a paradise quite familiar and yet eternally remote, and is so easy to understand and yet so inexplicable, is due to the fact that it reproduces all the emotions of our innermost being, but entirely without reality and remote from its pain."

By contrast, the "journey" metaphor of depth hinges upon direction and progress toward a goal. The surface is defined in terms of covering ground, while the content is the ground covered. The longer the path, the more ground is covered, and the more content is accumulated. This means that the metaphorical orientation of depth in the "journey" metaphor is very different from that in the "container" metaphor. While in the latter what is deeper (the core) is more basic or fundamental than the surface, in the former what is deeper is patently less obvious, denser, and more puzzling than what seemed at first. In the "journey" metaphor, points that are not on the surface are hidden from immediate view; we need to go into them in depth. This requires effort – digging or searching – to reveal them so that we can see them. As we go more deeply into matters, we reveal more on the surface, which allows us to see more, that is, to understand more. But the journey remains open-ended.

My overarching argument in this section, and in the next, is, simply put, that Wittgenstein discussion of music, from his middle period onward, evinces an ideational shift from the "container" metaphor of depth to the "journey" metaphor of depth. This positions Wittgenstein historically as a significant intermediary figure in the passage from Romanticism to contemporary philosophy of music – a forefather to some current turning of the tide in the field, as I shall argue in Section 5. Importantly, Wittgenstein's gravitating toward the "journey" metaphor is closely related to his thinking about language and logic at the time. Wittgenstein came to understand depth in terms of logical possibility. Deepening, seeing depth, takes the form of an increase in the valence and density of dimensions along which possibilities for characterization emerge for us; yet the work of characterization involves us, which means also the variety of failures to fashion a characterization that are possible.[71] According to Wittgenstein (BT §2), things (sentences, fiction stories, paintings, sloppy handwriting) acquire depth for us as we understand them. Wittgenstein's point is that these are not simply pieces of information in need of decoding, as if what they mean has already been placed and made visible within a space of possibility.[72] It is only by means of a certain phrasing that such things characterize anything at all.[73]

His final example in that section of the *Big Typescript* is particularly telling – reading a sentence with and without understanding. "Remember how it is," he

---

[71] See Floyd (2018a).

[72] Compare: "The way music speaks. Don't forget that even though a poem is composed in the language of information, it is not employed in the language-game of informing" (RPPI §888; Z §§160–161).

[73] This idea of depth is fully developed and applied directly to music in a later remark from 1946 (MS 130, 60–62), in which Wittgenstein discusses the end of the fourth movement (Allegretto) from Beethoven's Seventh Symphony. Like in the case of a sentence in a story (in the example

writes (BT §2, 9), "when you read a sentence with the wrong intonation [*Betonung*] and as a result you don't understand it, and then suddenly you discover how it ought to be read." Intonation (i.e., phrasing) brings in one's sense of the possibilities for human expression and human characterization. It also brings in the possibility and the choice of expanding this range within the purview of tuning-in relationships. In a later lecture (LC, 40), Wittgenstein offered a related example of reading poetry together. In the context of Wittgenstein's lecture, this was in fact his way of answering the explicit question, when someone plays a tune, what "getting it" consists in – what does it consist in to "get hold of the tune"? The reading example underscores how Wittgenstein's notion of depth is to be refracted from his corresponding discussions of reading with and without understanding vis-à-vis his pianola analogies around that time, and later. Most strikingly, this also anticipates Wittgenstein's fully mature treatment of the language-as-music simile in the *Philosophical Investigations* (PI §527ff), in particular as he ponders how one leads anyone to understand a poem or a theme: "Phrased like *this*, emphasized like this, heard in this way, this sentence is the beginning of a transition to *these* sentences, pictures, actions. (A multitude of familiar paths lead off from these words in all directions.)" (PI §534).

The "journey" metaphor of depth is in full display in the passage from Wittgenstein's letter to Koder (LK, 37–38). For Wittgenstein, understanding music is a journey toward acquaintance not only with possibilities for human expression and characterization, but also, and importantly, toward characterization of one's own humanity. That journey is goal-oriented, yet indeterminate and unending. Wittgenstein emphasizes the investigative nature of phrasing and rephrasing, as well as the daring choice to take on a specific phrasing as an invitation to traverse a whole field of possibilities in the hope of reaching one that would necessitate itself, that is, to see in the score something we have not seen before. Seeing depth is a matter of actively seeking out an articulation of possibilities, an increase in the range and density of possibilities, a richness of character that characterization yields, and the emerging of new, hitherto untapped possibilities for further characterization. The axis of verticality pertaining to musical understanding, extending from the structured surface of musical language toward inexhaustible gain, is no longer pseudo-spatial and irrational, as in the Romantic "container" metaphor, but logical – a matter of

---

from the *Big Typescript*), what the musical passage tells one – the significance of the gesture – depends on "stage setting," that is, its position within the variation, the position of the variation within the movement, the position of the movement within the symphony, and ultimately all this rests on its setting in the whole musical language to which it belongs. Cf. Z §173.

interrelations among language-game, as Wittgenstein realized in his later writings.[74]

3.3 Illuminating Comparisons

Wittgenstein's most philosophically dynamic remarks on music in his middle period occur in his lectures in Cambridge. The contexts for these remarks run the gamut from his own criticism of his erstwhile picture theory to discussions of language, logic, and the foundations of mathematics. This underscores my contention that Wittgenstein's thinking about, and through music has been connected right from the start primarily with logic and language, and not with aesthetics as commonly understood.[75] Moreover, as Hagberg (2014) noted, the distinctive progression in Wittgenstein's treatment of aesthetics in the middle period was to open it up, to broaden and deepen (in the aforementioned sense of a "journey") its concerns. He decisively interweaved the subject's various and variegated strands throughout his lectures and writing, expounding the layered interconnections between aesthetic considerations and every other area of philosophy on which he has set his mind.[76]

Still, it may come as no surprise that the two sets of lectures, which Wittgenstein dedicated to aesthetics, in 1933 (WLM, 9:1–50) and in 1938 (LC), feature intense explorations of musical matters, paying close attention in his examples to multiform techniques of characterization involved in mutual tuning-in relationships. Wittgenstein typifies aesthetic engagement as a site for trying out and establishing tuning-in relationships, as we offer descriptions, call attention to details and make comparisons, thereby bringing what is there to be seen into focus, for ourselves and for others. Toward the end of his 1933 set of lectures (WLM, 9:40–42), we find Wittgenstein revisiting his 1912–1913 experiments on rhythm, which I discussed in Section 2. The philosophical lesson, which he drew out from these experiments, concerned the open-ended, yet attentive, dynamics of comparing "illuminating notes" as opposed to the scientific idea that musical experiences trigger self-contained aesthetic responses, which we can collect as mere data points, recording the power of what we hear to bring about causal effects in us. Illuminating comparisons require a choice and an effort "to get it right" within the space of possibility, to

---

[74] I return to this in Section 4.2.

[75] Wittgenstein began his later set of lectures on aesthetics from 1938 by saying that "the subject (Aesthetics) is very big and entirely misunderstood as far as I can see" (LC I, 1). It is very big in the sense that aesthetics weaves itself through all of philosophy and its reach into human affairs is much greater than usually granted. It is entirely misunderstood in the sense that its concerns are completely removed from either empirical or essentialist questions.

[76] Noë (2023, Chapter 10) goes even further to contend that philosophy and aesthetics are bound together for Wittgenstein: philosophy aims at aesthetic integration and understanding.

show someone else and enable a response so that a new possibility or aspect may come to life.

Interestingly, in these lectures Wittgenstein explained the distinctive character of aesthetics by means of a contrast between experimental psychology and psychoanalysis. While psychology has "a tendency to explain away" (WLM, 9:39), "aesthetics like psychoanalysis doesn't explain anything away" (WLM, 9:45). The uniqueness of aesthetics lies in the nature of the explanations (reasons, justifications) that are offered and accepted in the attempt to address a given instance of aesthetic puzzlement: we are genuinely interested in, and care for "the actual verifying phenomena" (WLM, 9:43) of the parties involved – the onset for mutual tuning-in relationship. "Criterion of correctness of aesthetic analysis must be agreement of person to whom I make it. [. . .] [A]esthetics does not lie in finding a mechanism" (WLM, 9:46). Contrasting the modes of explanation in psychology and psychoanalysis allowed Wittgenstein to spell out the dynamic, productive, conversational, nonhypothetical, and therein immanently human character of aesthetics.

What is distinctive about aesthetic explanation is that it calls for reasons, not causes. "Aesthetic craving for an explanation is not satisfied by a hypothesis," he says: "This is what I mean by saying Aesthetics is not Psychology" (WLM, 9:39). "What is a reason in Aesthetics?" he asks: "A reason for having this word in this place rather than that; this musical phrase rather than that" (WLM, 9:30); "a reason consists in drawing your attention to something which removes an uneasiness" (WLM, 9:33). A reason, in this sense, addresses what presents itself as a necessity, an experience of meaning: for example, "Why is this note absolutely necessary?" (WLM, 9: 31). According to Wittgenstein (WLM, 9:31), we draw a possibility in, and characterize, by drawing comparisons, illuminating a field of possible projections of a concept and a potential development of the mode of characterization.

Characterization involves presenting phenomena, laid out side by side, independently of the causally determined sequence of events, in a creative, fitting order, which would "make a synopsis possible" (WLM, 9:31). In that sense, aesthetics is descriptive (WLM, 9:23). A comparison is an articulation of possibilities, which invites further comparisons and re-phrasings, serving and instancing possibilities for further characterization of what is there to be seen or heard. The open-endedness of the aesthetic engagement, its flow, is regulated by manifold, nuanced, never fixed or stable, patently incalculable "verifying phenomena" of the parties involved. These "verifying phenomena" afford ways in which we initiate and promote the looking, interrogating, comparing, noticing, and reminding, in which aesthetic inquiry consists. Wittgenstein's point is that in aesthetics there is always a sense in which "I can go on" (WLM, 9:29). This is quintessentially a pronouncement of the "journey" metaphor of depth. Yet success is never guaranteed.

The importance of aesthetics is found primarily not just in delineating and clarifying this mode of engagement, but also, and significantly, in Wittgenstein's urge to cultivate it. Fitting characterizations, when a solution to an aesthetic puzzle "speaks for itself," are important not only because they are always occur in situ, grounded in activity, embedded in context, and shaped by interest and situation, but also because they enact resemblances which unite a culture's ways of life. Mutual tuning-in relationships are not just a matter of doing, but significantly also a matter of making. Trying to find Keller in Brahms is a move in a practice of making perspicuous, displaying, unveiling, bringing out, and setting forth. Musicality is the ability to participate in this sort of practice.[77]

3.4 Aspects of Decline

Reorienting depth from "container" to "journey" problematized modern music for Wittgenstein, over and above his explicit dislike of these kinds of music. He admitted (CV, 8 [6]) that he approaches "what is called modern music with the greatest mistrust (without understanding its language)." At a time of cultural decline, the dissolution of the resemblances which unite a culture's ways of life results in myopia, in a difficulty to characterize, hence, in a difficulty to see depth, because characterization is entangled with a publicly available picture or model – Wittgenstein used the term "ideal" for this – of what is drawn in by the characterization and how it is supposed to look and feel.

For Wittgenstein (CV, 30 [26]), an ideal is "an object of comparison – a measuring rod as it were – within our way of looking at things." It allows for an overview for purpose of seeing something anew, a possibility that can be rendered in a comprehensible and communicable way: "you would need to describe the instances of the ideal in a sort of serial grouping" (WLA, 36). An aesthetic ideal is not some simple representational standard – a perceived token of something, or even a matter of fact – that directs us and which we try just to duplicate in our own artistic activity. Artistic achievement lies not in replicating a prototype, but in attuning ourselves to one another creatively by means of the ideal. Facilitating an aesthetic engagement, ideals are conducive to developing a cultured sense of taste, artistic sensibilities, and judgments that in turn manifest them. According to Wittgenstein (WLA, 37),

> When one describes changes made in a musical arrangement as directed to bringing the arrangement of parts nearer to an ideal, the idea is not before us like a straight line which is set before us when we try to draw it. (When

---

[77] See LC I:6.

questioned about what we are doing we might cite another tune which we thought not to be as near the ideal.) [. . .] To see how the ideal comes in, say in making the bass quieter, look at what is being done and at one's being dissatisfied with the music as it is.

"The ideal is the tendency of people who create such a thing," says Wittgenstein (WLM, 9:22), so to find what ideal we are oriented toward, we must look at what we do. Yet what we do, the practice, changes with the employment of ideals. Ideals loop down and change what they stand for. So, an ideal of a face or of a certain balance in polyphonic music changes with time, and yet each time we should say, "this is the ideal" (WLM, 9:19). We identify an ideal by virtue of some special role which it plays in the lives of certain people (WLM, 9:20).

This intrinsic relation between ideals and cultural cohesion makes them particularly sensitive to, and indicative of, changes in cultural conditions. Here Spengler's influence on Wittgenstein is very clear. The demise of aesthetic ideals is emblematic of a dissolution of the resemblances which unite a culture's ways of life – Wittgenstein (LC, I:7–11) speaks of a loss of interest in, and care for fine detail and origins regarding arts and crafts, settling for imitations – as it becomes more and more difficult to characterize the topography of culture by yielding an overview that can be rendered in a comprehensible and communicable way. For Wittgenstein, as for Spengler, culture at its height enables different people at different times and places to pool their cultural efforts and make use of their tasteful and creative powers in a common spiritual bond: "Culture is like a great organization which assigns to each of its members his place, at which he can work in the spirit of the whole, and his strength can with a certain justice be measured by his success as understood within that whole" (CV, 8–9 [6]). The time of civilization, meaning "age without culture," shows itself in the disintegration of culture into a host of disjointed efforts and nondiscriminating judgments. It is a breakdown of the cohesive forces formerly embodied both in the observance of a shared tradition and in the attempt to work in a common spirit. A disintegration of the similarities that would unite a culture's way of life by enabling human beings to express and experience something exalted or even sacred.

Wittgenstein's philosophical concern with myopia as a condition of cultural decline finds its expression in a nuanced treatment of modern music and its relation to the challenge of philosophizing in an age without culture. "General tendency of this age is to take away possibilities of expression [once a method is found]: which is characteristic of age without a culture," Wittgenstein told his students (WLM, 5:2). Philosophy is now "reduced to a matter of skill" (WLM, 5:2) – "[The] style of thinking has changed = nimbus of philosophy has been lost. [...] [T]here is no room for expression of personality" (WLM, 5:2). For Wittgenstein, the maxim of progress prescribes the relentless activity of constructing more and more complicated structures and "even clarity is only a means to this end & not an end in itself" (CV, 9 [7]). "For me," he wrote (CV, 9 [7]), "on the contrary clarity, transparency, is an end in itself. I am not interested in erecting a building but in having the foundations of possible buildings transparently before me."

Reflecting on the possibility for future music, Wittgenstein (MT, 49) wrote:[78]

> I shouldn't be surprised if the music of the future were in unison [*einstimmig*]. Or is that only because I cannot clearly imagine several voices? Anyway, I can't imagine that the old large forms (string quartet, symphony, oratorio, etc.) will be able to play any role at all. If something comes it will have to be – I think – simple, transparent. In a certain sense, naked. Or will this apply only to a certain race, only to one kind of music (?)

The passage is a composite of Spengler's ideas. For Spengler, the future always transcends the current epoch and it is always marked by a return to the simplest, most basic expression of life. Also, "pure civilization, as a historical process, consists in a taking-down of forms that have become inorganic or dead" (Spengler 1939, vol. 1, 31). However, in the context of Wittgenstein's idiosyncratic use of the optical metaphor of "transparency" as the opening up of the expressive possibility of a synopsis, that is, seeing connections by means of a perspicuous or surveyable representation (cf. PI §122), a return to simplicity means becoming reacquainted with the fluidity of simplicity, as explicated earlier in this section. The peculiar use of the metaphor of transparency betokens his increasing emphasis on the idea that music is physiognomic, intransitively transparent to human life. The idea of transparency as surveyability is diametrically opposed to what is prescribed by the form of progress: compulsive overstructuring and obfuscation, and, with it, a fragmentation into calculable objects that reduce the personal expression of human values to a method and a mechanism. Within the realm of Wittgenstein's optical metaphor, what I propose to call "myopia" is to be contrasted with transparency precisely in this sense.

The relevant senses of myopia are expounded in a few passages, which Wittgenstein dedicated to the modern music of his time. In a diary entry from January 27, 1931 (MS183, 59–61), Wittgenstein wrote:[79]

---

[78] The allusion, if it was intended at all, to the title of Richard Wagner's 1861 essay on the music of the future must be tongue in cheek. Also, it should be noted, Wittgenstein's use of the term "form" here is erroneous as pertaining to his examples, which are, from a musicological point of view, formats, rather than forms.

[79] My translation differs from the standard print edition. Cf. MT, 67–69. My translation preserves what I take as crucial semiotic ambiguities in Wittgenstein's original German.

> The music of all periods [insertion: the music of the past] always appropriates certain maxims of the good and the right of its own time. In this way we recognize the principles of Keller in Brahms etc etc. And for that reason [insertion: good] music, which is being conceived today or that has been conceived recently, which is therefore modern, seems absurd; for if it corresponds to any of the maxims that are articulated today, then it must be rubbish. This sentence is not easy to understand but it is so: no one is astute enough to formulate today what is correct, and all formulations, maxims, which are articulated are nonsense [*Unsinn*]. The truth would sound entirely paradoxical to all people. And the composer who feels this within him must confront with this feeling everything that is [insertion: now] articulated and therefore [his music] must appear by the present standards absurd, timid [*blödsinnig*]. But not absurd in a dressed-up sense (for after all, this is basically what corresponds to the present attitude) but vacuous [*nichtssagend*]. Labor is an example of this where he created something really significant as in some few pieces.

The passage opens with the assertion of the intrinsic connection between characterization and cultural cohesion as exemplified again, as in the passage from Wittgenstein's lecture quoted last in the previous section, by the suggestion to find Keller in Brahms. This is the onset for transparency and depth: being able to see the head in a puzzle picture. From this follows Wittgenstein's take on modern music as a problem of opacity, or myopia. The very idea of good modern music, that is, music that is intransitively transparent to human life in an age without culture, and in this sense authentic, seems to him absurd – an afterimage of an unseeable something. The transition to the modern shows itself in some sort of constraint – an inability to conceptualize that very transition. Wittgenstein's point is that there is something, for sure, to be grasped and expressed within cultural decline, but we are not astute enough to pronounce new ideals amid the breakdown of ideals. We have become constrained by the incommensurability that obtains between us and the past, and hence run up against a paradox: even if we knew "the truth," we probably would not be able to comprehend it.

Thus, the music that has become emblematic of cultural decline exhibits either of the two prevailing aspects of such absurdity. It is either nonsensical, or else vacuous. It is nonsensical when it abides with the pronounced maxim of progress, becoming absurd in a superficially attractive sense, which Wittgenstein refers to as "rubbish." As such it reflects a constraint on seeing that we do not comprehend. It is vacuous when it recoils from progress, becoming absurd in the laughable sense for its timidity, for not having the verve for passing as absurd in the other "dressed-up" sense. It is not "dressed-up," yet also not "naked" in the sense Wittgenstein utilized in his remark on the music of the future. As such it reflects a constraint on seeing what we do not comprehend, on seeing through.

Wittgenstein's analysis maps very closely onto the common distinction between progressive romantics and classicist epigones in early-twentieth-century music, which we find also in Spengler and Schenker.[80] Yet, contrary to both Spengler and Schenker, Wittgenstein leaves the door open for a good, namely, authentic modern music, appropriate to an age without culture. Spengler (1939, vol. 1, 32) maintained that civilization, as the most external and artificial state of which evolved humanity is capable, is the inevitable, irreversible destiny of culture. It is death following life. Schenker, on the contrary, maintained that composers ought to actively seek to reverse the decline by setting forth his theories as a guide to composers and performers alike.[81]

Wittgenstein's independent third alternative shows, I argued elsewhere (Guter 2015), a hybrid notion of musical decline, in which historical inevitability and spiritual rejuvenation are not necessarily mutually exclusive. Wittgenstein detected in Schenker' theory the same mistake of confusing "prototype" and "object," which he diagnosed in Spengler.[82] This undercuts Schenker's hope for cultural rejuvenation by means of some concrete, hence dogmatic return to the compositional practices of yore, yet lending an ear to depth need not abide with the kind of spatial verticality of the "container" variety, which Schenker's theory showcases.

The conundrum of good modern music became pressing for Wittgenstein as he linked it intimately with the challenge of philosophizing amid cultural decline, which was deeply personal for him.[83] This is already suggested when Wittgenstein (MS183, 60) voices his worry about the prospect of good modern music that "no one is astute enough to formulate today what is correct [. . .] The truth would sound entirely paradoxical to all people." Here he seems to echo Spengler's (1939, vol. 1, 42) similar worry that the philosophers of his present day did not have a real standing in actual life, that they had not acquired the necessary reflective understanding of the time or its many built-in limitations, which philosophizing in time of civilization requires.

---

[80] See Guter (2015).   [81] See Cook (1989, 428).   [82] See my discussion in Section 3.1.

[83] The intimate connection, in Wittgenstein's mind, between composing music and philosophical style is everywhere present in the background during his middle-period, from his 1930 diary entry (MT, 17–19), where he wrote, "I often think that the highest I wish to achieve would be to compose a melody," through his musings on the difference between composing with a pen on paper and by hearing within (in relation to Brahms and Bruckner), to his jotting down a musical fragment (known as the "Leidenschaftich theme" – see CV, 19 [21]) and relating it to his "destructive" work on philosophy. See full discussion of these and other related instances in Guter and Guter (2023).

The conundrum of good modern music became pressing for Wittgenstein also because he intimately, yet explicitly linked his own prospects as a philosopher in an age without culture to the creative efforts of Gustav Mahler, the only truly modern composer, who was worthy of attention in his eyes. Wittgenstein's attitude toward Mahler exhibits an admixture of hatred (of his music) and admiration (of his musicianship), which was quite typical of his Viennese background.[84] Yet, Wittgenstein's harshly critical remarks on Mahler attest that his music did not fit in Wittgenstein's distinction between nonsensical and vacuous modern music.[85] Wittgenstein (CV, 17 [20]) offers a Spenglerian observation that a Mahler symphony might be a work of art of a totally different sort, embodying an entirely different kind of spiritual enterprise, for which our aesthetic measuring rods are inadequate. His critique is not that Mahler's music is nonsensical or vacuous, but rather that it fails to be authentic, especially when he belabors to show his allegiance to the old musical tradition (MT, 93). According to Wittgenstein, Mahler's myopia is a form of self-deception. "Lying to oneself about one's own inauthenticity, must have a bad effect on one's style," Wittgenstein (MS120, 72 v) wrote, "for the consequence will be that one is unable to distinguish what is genuine and what is false. This is how the inauthenticity of Mahler's style may be explained and I am in the same danger."

In a sense, his frustration at Mahler appears to stem from a realization that the prodigious composer had ultimately fallen short of creating music that is authentic to his time due to his self-deception. This frustration is self-directed, and the last remark (CV, 76–77 [67]), written shortly before Wittgenstein's death, only shows how deep and unresolved this double-edged frustration has grown. Wittgenstein contends that one cannot see oneself from within an overview, and therefore, one can always (mistakenly) render one's stylistic otherness as some sort of excellence. "Even someone who struggles against vanity, but not entirely successfully, will always deceive himself about the value of what he produces" (CV, 77 [67]).

Ultimately, the problem afflicting Mahler as a composer, and Wittgenstein as a philosopher and writer, is a problem of incommensurability, which pertains to the cultural presuppositions for making value distinctions in the first place: "If today's circumstances are really so different, from what they once were, that

---

[84] See Schorske (1999, Chapter 11). Wittgenstein's genuine admiration for Mahler's conducting endured throughout his entire life. See CV, 43 [38]; LR, 133–134.

[85] Wittgenstein's four remarks on Mahler belong to different periods. Two (MT, 93; CV, 17 [20]) were written in the early middle-period: one (MS120, 72v) in 1937 and the last one (CV, 76–77 [67]) a decade later. However, the entire set shows a remarkable consistency of tone and substance.

you cannot compare your work with earlier works in respect of its genre, then you equally cannot compare its value with that of the other work" (CV, 77 [67]). Amid cultural decline one cannot tell for sure whether culture continues, leaving one behind, or whether culture has disappeared, but no one else can notice it. "I myself am constantly making the mistake under discussion," Wittgenstein (CV, 77 [67]) admitted. This is an uneasy realization for a philosopher who, in a sense, has set himself on a journey to combat decline by rectifying the maladies of philosophy with his own interlocutory style of clarification by means of entering mutual tuning-in relationships.

4 The Late Period: Knowing Human Beings

4.1 Musicality in Language

The master simile of language as music, which I explored in Section 1.3, culminated in *Philosophical Investigations* (PI §527). The suggestion that "understanding a spoken sentence is closer than one thinks to what is ordinarily called understanding a musical theme," which was asserted fully fledged already in the *Brown Book* (BB, 167), is set to oppose the persistent idea, which the *Investigations* as whole is designed to disentangle, that understanding a sentence is knowing the meanings, namely, the references, of its individual words. Instead, Wittgenstein advances the idea that "understanding a sentence is hearing the music that shapes its life," to use Cavell's words (Cavell 2022, 280).

This pulls together many strings, which I singled out in my discussion over the preceding sections. Hearing the music that shapes the life of a sentence, tuning-in onto the "'soul' of the words" (PI §530), that is, having a reason for embracing a particular phrasing, which necessitates itself, letting the gesture "creep into my life [as] I make it my own" (CV, 83), show a clear emphasis on speech, namely, on the fluidity of countless techniques of characterization in which human communicability inheres, and on the open-ended, humanly textured dynamics of making illuminating comparisons, on justifying them, accepting, or rejecting them. Musicality is shown in the emphasis on the ability to characterize and the importance of the specific ways we characterize, including the choices and the risks that we take in characterizing, to the extent that lacking the ability to experience the meaning of words, namely, aspect or meaning-blindness, is comparable to lacking a musical ear.[86] Here we may observe the complete overcoming in Wittgenstein's later philosophy of his erstwhile commitment to elide musicality, which I explicated in Section 2.

---

[86] See PPF, xi: 225 §260; LWI §783.

The "anthropological view" brought into prominence the idea that understanding a gesture requires looking at how the gesture relates to the form of life of which it is a part. That is, a gesture has a point only in human life. We must look at the environment, the surroundings, where the language functions – the complex form of life that is revealed in the way we speak and act. The importance of the distinct axis in Wittgenstein's philosophical progression pertaining to his allusions to mechanical means of musical reproduction, which I discussed in Section 1.2, lies in the present context, in which Wittgenstein focuses again on differences between understanding and not-understanding, precisely in the realization, which bounces off examples like the pianola, that the tempting idea that the concept of understanding describes, or prescribes the state of some internal mechanism misses the way understanding connects with ongoing, complex and open-ended patterns of performance – Wittgenstein eventually dubbed these "patterns of life" (LWI §211)[87] – within a horizon of previous training, manifest abilities and forms of responsiveness.

Many of Wittgenstein's later remarks on music (e.g., Z §§155–175) underscore the point that understanding music has nothing to do with anything that happens at the time of its being attributed. Hearing music with understanding is quite a different experience from hearing music without understanding. One understands a melody, as one understands an utterance, while one hears it, but understanding is not an accompaniment of hearing, and it is not reducible to any sensation of feeling that may accompany hearing or playing music. Understanding is not an experience that goes on concurrently with the hearing. Nor is it a process of any kind that accompanies listening to music. For Wittgenstein, this is as nonsensical as saying that expressive playing, which is a manifestation of understanding what one plays, is an accompaniment of the music. Understanding music is understanding a language, and so expressive playing and being able to explain it to another person, require a culture. The expression "I experienced that passage quite differently" does not indicate anything that occurred in oneself while listening. Rather it tells one "what happened" only if one is "at home in the special conceptual world that belongs to these situations" (Z §164).

In the train of thought that immediately follows the pronouncement of the language-as-music simile (PI §§528–535), Wittgenstein sets up his discussion by utilizing two imaginary cases, which he contrasts in a mutually reflecting way. One is the case of a language-like phenomenon ("speaking with tongues") in which the mere play of sounds or intonation can be conceived as laden with meaning (cf. Z §151). Of course, says Wittgenstein (Z §161), "there is a strongly

---

[87] I discuss this further in Section 4.3.

musical element in verbal language. [...] [A]ll the innumerable *gestures* made with the voice." But these are aspects of speech, a matter of phrasing and characterizing, just like speech-like aspects of certain types or genres of music and manners of performing music (cf. CV, 40 [34]; 71 [62]). The case of "speaking with tongues" is a converse parody to the one, which Wittgenstein shares (Z §161), of a person who is under the impression that the expressive playing of a Chopin piece is a coded message, whose meaning is kept secret from him. Wittgenstein's point, I take it, is that neither parody does justice to "the way music speaks" (Z §160; cf. PI §529).

The other case concerns a language "in whose use the 'soul' of the words played no part." Users of such a language are blind to any necessitation of characterizing, which is not fully derived from the position of words in accordance with explicit rule and tables (PI §530; cf. Z §145; 147–148; PG, 171–172). In such language words have no physiognomy and each word can be replaced by another arbitrary one of the user's own invention. Every sentence would need to be decoded to get an impression of it.[88] Wittgenstein's instructive point is that no stories can be written in such language. It allows for no stage-setting; hence it is blind with respect to Wittgenstein's reoriented concept of depth, which I discussed in Section 3.2. Such a language would befit a form of linguistic life that left no space for linguistic play. Such form of life would be radically unlike our human lives with language (RPPI §324).

These contrasting imaginary cases bookend the language-as-music simile in two important senses. First, Wittgenstein's concept of understanding is fluid. It ranges over the two imaginary poles, and everything in between, admitting degrees of understanding and different kinds of understanding (PI §532). Yet precisely here the distinct directionality of the language-as-music simile shows its mettle as Wittgenstein again puts onus on entering mutual tuning-in relationships as in the case of leading someone to comprehending a poem or a musical theme by phrasing it in a particular way, thereby seeing necessity and depth in it in a living way (PI §§533–534; cf. LC, 40). In such cases, one cannot get away with a mere paraphrase. Illuminating comparisons must be offered, and, if successful, also accepted and engaged with.

Reflecting on the "queerness" of hearing a word in a particular sense – that is *experiencing* its meaning, hence moving beyond the idea of meaning as use – Wittgenstein (PI §534) ties together the idea of aesthetic puzzlement as the onset for enquiry, hence as the prompt for further characterization, with the "journey" metaphor of depth, in a way which corresponds to his portrayal of

---

[88] Wittgenstein (MS161, 6f) suggested that a chemical symbolism is an example for such "soulless" language.

emerging voices while phrasing a musical passage in his 1930 letter to Koder (LK, 37–38): "A multitude of familiar paths lead off from these words in all directions" (PI §534). The previous occurrence of the same assertion in PI §525 strikingly connects this train of thought with the very same example which Wittgenstein used in the *Big Typescript* (BT §2, 7) to flesh out how seeing possibilities and characterization are involved in the way a sentence in a story acquires depth for the reader. Wittgenstein's point remains that entering the game is an ineliminable part of making a word come alive for us as we chart the dense contexts within which speech makes its specific sense.

Even more strikingly, this segment of the discussion rounds up with yet another evocation of the puzzlement involved in feeling the ending of a church mode as an ending (PI §535). This comes full circle with Wittgenstein's profound lesson from his 1912–1913 experiments on rhythm,[89] as this was the exact same example, which he used then for the first time to explain to his students (WLM, 9:41) what he was looking for at the laboratory yet failed to accomplish. In that 1933 lecture Wittgenstein fully answered the question, "what happens we learn to *feel* the ending of a church mode as an ending?" (PI §535) – we have been shown ways to characterize what we hear, such as, Wittgenstein suggested, by comparing with similar things in our modern keys or by leaving out the tonic in a modern key, thereby becoming aware of our tonally hierarchical "mental presets," which are embedded in, and embodied by common-practice era music. Wittgenstein's point is that musicality also inheres in the ability to unlearn, hence, to hear anew. This is now applied to language. And, as I argued in Section 2, this was taken squarely from Stumpf and Myers.[90]

The second important sense in which the two imaginary cases – "speaking with tongues" and the "soulless" language – inform the language-as-music simile remains implicit in the *Philosophical Investigations*. The simile is a mediator, or a median between the two imaginary poles also in the sense that musicality is taken as a ligature to understanding. In that sense, Wittgenstein in fact not only remains uncommitted to drawing a line between music and language, but also makes it palpably clear that such a line cannot be underpinned in any stable, that is, theoretical way. As Bowie (2007, 18) pointed out, "the resources for drawing the line, that is, language itself, may not be sufficient to describe the musical 'side' of the line, which has to be experienced in ways language cannot circumscribe." Thus, writes Wittgenstein (CV, 60 [52]), "the [musical] theme interacts with language," thereby rendering the axis of verticality pertaining to musical understanding, extending from the

---

[89] See my discussion in Section 2.1.   [90] See also Guter (2024).

structured surface of the music toward all that could be experienced in ways language cannot circumscribe, as logical, namely, a matter of interrelations among language-games.[91]

Wittgenstein (CV, 54 [47]) singled out the myopic nature of the patently generalized formal-analytic outlook that serves to compartmentalize melodies (and other musical structures) in terms of such elements as successions of tones and changes of keys. Trivially, within the scope of Western common-practice-era music, all these elements, indeed, "appear in coordination," that is, in accord with the hierarchic configuration of Western tonal music. However, this falls short of explaining what enlivens music for us. For this requires broaching the multifarious interrelated language games that constitute "the rhythm of our language, of our thinking and feeling" (CV, 59 [52]) – the living, embodied "origin" of the melody, which in itself, as he says, is *not yet* a melody – and the gesture that is incorporated into our human lives as if in a ceremony – the "role" that the melody plays, which is melody *no more*, but part of the lived, embodied realities of musical intelligibility.

4.2 Interrelated Language-Games

Wittgenstein's overarching response to the Romantic view of musical depth aligns with his emphasis on secondary language games and their embeddedness in a form of life, as he explores the territory of aspect perception, physiognomy, and the experience of meaning in his later writing. Such emphasis is clearly flagged in the train of thought immediately following the pronouncement of the language-as-music simile in the *Philosophical Investigations* (PI §§534–539), becoming full-fledged in the so-called second part of the *Investigations* (PPF), in *Zettel* and all his various late-vintage writings on the philosophy of psychology.[92] According to Wittgenstein, not all language games function on the same logical level: some language games presuppose familiarity with other language games. A move in a secondary language game can only be understood against the backdrop of the correlate move in a logically prior game.[93] "If I say [about a musical theme] e.g.," Wittgenstein wrote (CV, 59 [52]), "it's as if here a conclusion were being drawn, or, as if here something were being confirmed, or, as if *this* were a reply to what came earlier, – then the way I understand it

---

[91] The radical idea that "language trails off into what no longer would be called language" (VW, 395) appeared already in 1929 under the influence of Stumpf and Myers, as I argue in Guter (2024).

[92] Wittgenstein's distinction between different language games along these lines in such contexts, and his understanding that secondary language games play a more important role in ordinary communication than is generally thought, received considerable scholarly attention. See Hintikka and Hintikka (1986), Hintikka and Hintikka (1996), Hark (1990), Mulhall (1990).

[93] See PPF §274ff [PI, xi, 216ff]; LWI §795ff).

clearly presupposes familiarity with conclusions, confirmations, replies, etc." Such interrelations between language games are vertical in a logical sense.[94] In vertically interrelated language-games we could not explain to anyone such a secondary move without having acquired the primary one, "and this impossibility is a logical one" (LWI §803). One could avail oneself only of making comparisons, which may employ moves – verbal definitions or paradigmatic examples – in the language game that is being presupposed.

Wittgenstein recaptured and reimagined the Romantic emphasis on the ineffable specificity of the musical surface. As I pointed out in Section 3, whereas Romantic thinkers were committed to the "container" metaphor of musical depth and thus conceived of the ineffable specificity of the musical surface in terms of rationally unknowable interiority, Wittgenstein (CV, 59 [51–52]) replaced this semi-spatial notion of verticality with a logical sense of verticality in terms of interrelated language games. Musical depth is now fully portrayed as a journey from the structured surface of music onto the open-ended, indeterminate, manifold, dynamic vistas of the totality of our actual and possible language games. It is not perpendicular to the musical surface but, rather, spread over the surface of our practices and connects it with the complex and involved filigree-shaped patterns of our characteristic form of life. Yet importantly, as Mulhall (1990, 50) points out, such interrelations between language games – indeed, what I suggested calling "musicality in language" in the previous section – "confer patterning upon language as a whole, providing a means for achieving an *Ubersicht* which can aid one's mastery of language."

Reflecting on "the way music speaks" (RPPI §888; Z §160), Wittgenstein abides by the mature formulation of the language-as-music simile as he conflates, once again, understanding music and hearing the music that shapes the life of a sentence in language. He reminds the reader: "Don't forget that even though a poem is composed in the language of information, it is not used in the language-game of giving information" (Z §160). The way music speaks inheres in vertically interrelated language games. Its gestures, and how one reciprocates them, which enliven music for us, give rise to an opportunity for seeking intimacy with others. The gestures are not offered and reciprocated "to inform the other person," but rather to "find one another," which also means finding oneself (RPPI §874).[95] One is lost on another (or on oneself), if one fails to comprehend the patterning

---

[94] Ter Hark (1990) suggests contrasting this notion of verticality qua relations between different language games to a notion of horizontality qua a relation between a concept and a language game. He (Hark 1990, 34) puts the difference succinctly by saying that while all concepts are embedded horizontally in their respective language games, some are also embedded in a vertical relation to other language games.

[95] The translation of the reflexive verb *sich finden* as "finding one another" and "finding oneself" is mine.

that vertical interrelatedness confer upon language as a whole, coming to believe that the musical gesture is an inaccessible piece of information. Such is the parody on the person who mistook a Chopin piece for a coded message (RPPI §888; Z §161).

The resistance of the musical gesture to paraphrasing does not denote a tension between the knowable and the unknowable, as Romantic thinkers held, but rather the tension between different kinds of understanding, as he noted in the *Investigations* (PI §§531–532). Yet such recalcitrance is not a deficiency. For Wittgenstein, the way music speaks is transparent because its gestures are physiognomic, intransitively transparent to human life through a myriad of interrelated language games.[96] This notion of transparency allows Wittgenstein (CV, 59 [52]) to make the seemingly contradictory claim that "there just *is* no paradigm other than the theme. And yet again there *is* a paradigm other than the theme: namely the rhythm of our language, of our thinking & feeling." Indeed, we may say that "what this musical theme tells me is itself" (PI §524; cf. BB, 166; 178). Yet, "the question is really," says Wittgenstein (RPPI §36), "are these notes not the *best* expression for what is expressed [in the musical phrase]? Presumably. But that does not mean that they aren't to be explained by working on their surroundings." A clearer understanding of what the phrase means is available to us, but "this understanding would be reached by saying a great deal about the surroundings of the phrase" (RPPI §34). But this means that the structured face of the music, as it is being characterized, phrased, and rephrased, reveals the ineliminable uptake of interrelations between language games, evinced by multiform ways of characterizing, ultimately broaching "the whole field of our language games" (CV, 59 [52]). As Mulhall (1990, 50) puts it, "the question of the degree to which the logical geography of a language is run through with and given unity by such similarities between linguistic structures is not one which can be answered a priori."

In this sense, according to Wittgenstein (CV, 59–60 [51–52]), "the theme is a *new* part of our language, it becomes incorporated in it; we learn a new *gesture*. The theme interacts with language." By this conspicuous conflation of the two notions of a "paradigm" we see how the later Wittgenstein comes full

---

[96] See my discussion of Wittgenstein's notion of transparency in Section 3.4. I should add that it is for this reason, among others, that I find the tendency to associate Wittgenstein's later philosophy with Arnold Schoenberg's twelve-tone music, most notably by Cavell (2022), to be quite erroneous. Wittgenstein's notion of transparency is diametrically opposed to Schoenberg's notion of comprehensibility in composing with twelve-tones, which approximates Wittgenstein's imaginary case of a "soulless" language. In a sense, from a Wittgensteinian point of view, Schoenberg's twelve-tone music is music for the meaning-blind. See my full argument in Guter (2011) and Guter (forthcoming).

circle with what the earlier Wittgenstein was bound to elide, as I argued in Section 2.[97] He has come to fully acknowledge and appreciate the philosophical importance of paying close attention to all the deep-seated complex human competencies and activities, which extend to the very capability of language itself.

4.3 The Face of the Human

The ideational trajectory of "music in relation to concepts of the inner," which I discussed last in Section 3.1, reaches its apex in Wittgenstein's discussion of our knowledge of human beings or people (Menschenkenntnis) (PPF §355ff [PI, xi, 227ff]). Romantic thinkers began to imagine an interiority to music similar in its uncanniness to the interiority of the listening subject. Music gained an exalted status among the arts as a conduit for intimate knowledge of the inner. Wittgenstein clearly upheld such admiration of music, which he shared with thinkers who immediately influenced him – namely, Schopenhauer, Spengler, and Schenker – yet in the advent of his reorientation of musical depth, the relation of music to the realm of the inner turned into a journey onto the indefinite, ornamental expanse of "the bustle of human life" (RPPII §§624– 29). The Romantic emphasis on the indescribable specificity of musical expression turned into an emphasis on specific techniques of characterization which necessitate on a given occasion a certain possibility within an indefinite space of interrelated language games. The master simile of language-as-music morphed into a spearhead in Wittgenstein's push beyond the inner/outer picture (PI §§536–539).

Wittgenstein (CV, 59 [52]) harks back to his primary intuition of understanding aspects as faces when he writes that "a [musical] theme, no less than a face, wears an expression." As Floyd (2018a, 371) puts it, "a face has character, is a dense field of significance, perhaps (as has been argued) the densest field of significance we are capable of appreciating." Wittgenstein's later writings are replete with passages, in which he explores aspects in relation to characterization of musical and facial expressions.[98] His (CV, 94 [84]; cf. PI §285) point about "soulful expression in music," is that "it is not to be described in terms of degrees of loudness & of tempo. Any more than is a soulful facial expression describable in terms of the distribution of matter in space." Rather, "expression consists for us <in> incalculability" (CV, 83 [73]).

---

[97] Cf. CV, 94 [82]. Wittgenstein downplays the notion of "paradigm" in its equivocated sense altogether.

[98] See, e.g., PI §536; PPF §226 [PI. xi, 209]; CV, 96 [84]; LWI §§735, 739–41, 749, 754; LWII, 90. See also the discussion of these passages in relation to Wittgenstein's original musical fragment (Figure 4) in Guter and Guter (2023).

According to Wittgenstein, enormous variability, irregularity, and unpredictability are an essential part of human physiognomy and the concepts of the "inner" for which human physiognomy serves as basis (RPPII §§614–615; 617; 627). Human physiognomy is fundamentally nonmechanical; that is, it cannot be recognized or described by means of rules, and it introduces an indefiniteness, a certain insufficiency of evidence, into our physiognomic recognition that is constitutive; hence, it is not indicative of any deficiency of knowledge. This is precisely where the opposition between the notion of musicality, which weaves through Wittgenstein's entire philosophical progression, and what I described in Section 1.2 as the axis of allusions to mechanical means of musical reproduction in his writings comes to a head most vividly and most fruitfully. Exact, definite calculation and prediction is conceptually detrimental to what we normally regard as human expression (CV, 83–4 [73]; cf. PI §285; RPPII §§614–15).

Our concepts of the "inner" are constituted by indeterminate nuances of behavior, which are grounded in "patterns of life" (LWI §211). These are recurring, yet ever shape-shifting behavioral, facial, and verbal expressions that are innumerable and interwoven with a myriad of other such patterns, which we apprehend as structuring regularities within our life and thus designate by using certain words. The ensuing incalculability regarding expression means that the concept of "certainty" is dissociated from the concept of "proof" as "sufficient evidence passes over into insufficient without a borderline" (RPPII §614). The rules of evidence appropriate to empirical facts do not apply in our mutual tuning-in relationships.[99] The vertical shift in interrelated games of musical expression admits indeterminacy, which is constitutive of such games. This indefiniteness is in the nature of the language game played, a mark of its admissible evidence (LWI §888; RPPII §683; Z §374), which, according to Wittgenstein, is significantly unlike the kind of evidence used to establish scientific knowledge – it is what he calls "imponderable evidence" (PPF §§358–360 [PI, xi, 228]).

According to Wittgenstein (PPF §360 [PI, xi, 228]), "imponderable evidence includes subtleties of glance, of gesture, of tone." It consists in a mixture of immediate certainty and indeterminacy that characterizes our perception and understanding of other people's emotions, expressions, feelings, reactions, intentions, and thoughts. A proficient knower of human beings is endowed with a sensibility for the face of the human, a capacity in perceiving and judging the nature, moods, dispositions, and states of mind of other human beings, which to a certain extent we can teach one another. Knowledge of human beings

---

[99] Wittgenstein learned this lesson already early on during his 1912–1913 experiments on rhythm, as I argued in the previous sections.

can be learnt and taught by some, yet only through experience or varied observation and by exchanging "tips." It evades general formulations and carries consequences "of a diffuse kind." And while there are rules involved in intimating and acquiring such knowledge, "they do not form a system, and only experienced people can apply them rightly. Unlike calculating rules" (PPF §355 [PI, xi, 227]; cf. LWI §921). To be skillful, one needs to immerse oneself in the infinite variation of human physiognomy.

Blindness to subtleties of glance, of gesture, of tone is symptomatic of a loss of interest in our experience as we become more sedate in taking in the world – as if the entire field of our language games has been long been surveyed and successfully delineated. This is the kind of aspect or meaning-blindness, which Wittgenstein (PPF §§254–261 [PI, xi, 213–214]) compared to a lack of musical ear. Wittgenstein's point is that they are both not unimaginable as a human possibility at all. It is the sort of common "laziness" that shies one away from becoming acquainted with all those "inner voices" (namely, possibilities of characterization), which Wittgenstein conceded in his 1930 letter to Koder (LK, 37–38). It can be overcome. One has a choice to engage. More importantly, one ought to overcome it if one wishes to know more and more about oneself (as a human being).

Knowing human beings, as pertaining to making music, involves what I (Guter 2023a) call "game incorrigibility" – the phenomenon of "getting something right," which Wittgenstein (LC, 40) described in his example of reading a poem together as "being certain of yourself, reading it in *one way only*." In that scenario, this happens after one is being called on to reciprocate another way of reading the stanza. It is as if in this moment of "getting it right" we are caught, or we catch ourselves, in the act of characterizing. Interestingly, Wittgenstein's musical examples for game incorrigibility revolve primarily around the thorny question concerning choosing the right tempo in perform-ance: reading a sentence in the right tempo (CV, 65 [57]), finding out that nowadays the right tempo for a piece of music is different from its original metronome marking (Z §37), observing that changing a tempo affects the character of the musical theme (CV, 84 [74]), questioning when it is right to play a piece exactly according to the metronome (CV, 85 [75]; 92 [80]).[100]

In what seems to be an underdeveloped discussion at the end of section xi of PPF, Wittgenstein's examples for game incorrigibility mostly concern pain behavior, which are primary physiognomic language games.[101] The questions, "How does a man learn to get an 'eye' for something? And how can this eye be

---

[100] See in-depth discussion of these passages in Guter (2019b).
[101] See Hintikka and Hintikka (1986, 258).

used?" (PPF §361 [PI, xi, 228]) remain hanging in the air. Yet this is an instructive foil for considering what this means in interrelated physiognomic language games of the sort we get in musical expression. The natural expression of pain and the accompanying sensation language, which also involves other people's reaction to these expressions (PI §§289; 310), are grammatically inseparable from the experience of pain. Thus, there is no way of doubting what happens in such language games without transgressing them. One cannot separate the experience of pain from the expression of pain (PI §§250; 288; LWI §203). Such a challenge would presuppose an independent link between one's language and the world, one that bypasses these language games.

Yet contrary to the case of (genuine) pain, the aesthetic question of "getting it right" not only makes sense, but also is crucial. When a brain-splitting toothache strikes, there is no sense in speaking of "getting it right" – there is simply no way of "getting it wrong." This difference does not mean that the expressive gesture can be separated from the music played; this would not make sense. Wittgenstein explicitly maintained that one could repeat the expression that "accompanied" a tune without singing it with no more success than one could repeat the understanding that "accompanied" a sentence without saying it (PI §332; LC, IV: 29). But the point is, as Wittgenstein made it so clear already in his letter to Koder (LK, 37–38), that in making music there is always a possibility of becoming aware that we got it wrong. In fact, he contends, it is normally the opening move in such games: "you play [the music] and thereby notice distinctly that you play it and the passages still without understanding." An element of misunderstanding (in the sense of "not yet understanding," hence, in need of exploring further), and with it also an element of choice, is built into such interrelated physiognomic language games. In such precious moments of failure, or lacking, or disorientation, as Noë (2023, 99–100) puts it, "we are thrown back on ourselves and we need actually to make an effort to know where we are, what is going on, what matters. We need to labor to bring the world into focus."

The game could be rendered incorrigible insofar as our labor is rewarded by "getting it right." This "getting it right" is part of the game, that is, it is not a transgression of the game, as would have been the case with genuine pain behavior. But it is a fragile affair; for nothing can compel attunement with others. As we genuinely strive toward the aesthetic apex of game incorrigibility, we become more accomplished in knowing human beings. We find ourselves and one another in making music. Yet this Forsterian moment of "only connect!" leaves no room for the concept of "doubt" and, hence, no room either for discursive knowledge about matters of fact. No deficiency of knowledge has been addressed or rectified. The discovery, the disclosure, the articulation itself, arises out of characterizing, that is, seeing anew and appreciating the ways in which what has been exposed to view all along fits together or rises to meaningfulness, rather than in the discovery of new information. For that reason, Wittgenstein (CV, 80–81 [70]) thought that it is far from being obvious that one could describe what it means to say that "understanding music is a manifestation of human life."[102] One is required to come up with illuminating comparisons, drawing on the musicality of language to explain what music is.

5 The Paradigm Shift

In my introduction I posed a double-edged question about Wittgenstein and music. Regarding Wittgenstein's admitted concern to Maurice Drury that without appreciating the importance of music for him, his writings might be misunderstood, I set out to trace and explore how Wittgenstein harnessed musical examples, topics, and images to test, refine, and develop his philosophical views. Yet the philosophical importance that Wittgenstein saw in music is also a foil to articulating its otherness vis-à-vis convictions and debates that typify current analytically inclined philosophy of music. The title of this section betokens my twofold answer to this double-edged question. It is twofold because Wittgenstein's paradigm shift can be taken as being intrinsic to his philosophical development, but also as conducive (in its mature form) to matters, which are external to his work, albeit by way of contrast and refraction. Strangely, I take it, Wittgenstein's seems to be more a philosopher of music in the former sense, which pertains to the deepening of a certain philosophical sensitivity, than in the latter, professionally established sense. In the words of Cavell (2022, 280), "if language as such has for some reason become compromised in its powers of reference and expression [. . .] how can words satisfy us in our descriptions of our experience of music, which itself reflects the condition or fate of human speech? This seems to me a question worth occupying something to be called a philosophy of music."

Wittgenstein's (CV, 59 [52]) final "tale of two paradigms" from 1946 encapsulates what I would call the intrinsic shift. It is the logical shift from a focus on sentential form to opening up onto the form of life, from absolute simplicity to fluid simplicity as evinced by the primacy of what I proposed to call "mutual tuning-in relationships," an experience of characterizing "the rhythm of our language, of our thinking & feeling" within which one's conduct becomes meaningful to the partner tuned in on him. The two senses of "paradigm" (CV, 59 [52]) are like parentheses around his philosophical progression from before the *Tractatus* to the *Philosophical Investigations* and beyond. Eventually he needs them both. But along the way he had to let go of the ideal of simplicity

---

[102] I modified the translation.

as an absolute. The master simile of language-as-music was conducive to his quest for fluidity. The simile brings to the fore all that is fluid, nonmechanical, embedded in ways of life, incalculable and indeterminate in language, first and foremost gesture and expression. It afforded Wittgenstein a spring of powerful analogies, images, and after-images for his career-long philosophical exploration of meaning and understanding, and most pertinently, the communicability of aspects. For him, there was no point in thinking about music without specific characterization, no point in thinking about musical sound apart from its embeddedness in a specific human gesture and its many elaborations in thought, speech and feeling, that is, apart from what Wittgenstein considered to be the preconditions, the lived, embodied realities, of musical intelligibility.

If it stands to reason, as Floyd (2018b) argues, that in his mature thought Wittgenstein successfully managed to embed logic in life, rendering logic ubiquitous in terms of criteria and procedures in our everyday lives, then we may conclude that the master simile of language-as-music was conducive to this philosophical maturation, as Wittgenstein's investigations of these criteria and procedures "show us the roles of voicing and speaking, of habit and questioning, the lives of words and ourselves with them as part of reality" (Floyd 2018b, 68). Mutual tuning-in relationships with their modular treatment of human procedures, actions, claims, choices, and persuasions become paramount – hence "understanding music is a manifestation of human life" (CV, 80 [70]), wherein logic is embedded. This is Wittgenstein's reoriented sense of depth as a journey, which is equally musical and logical.

Wittgenstein's subterranean intervention in the Romantic take on musical depth, as he weaved its original impetus into his forward-looking thinking about the philosophic entanglements of logic, language, and the mind, resulted in a pioneering philosophic outlook on music, which has remained largely incommensurate with some deep-seated convictions and proclivities still pronounced in contemporary analytic philosophy of music. Most obviously, Wittgenstein gravitated toward what has nowadays been dubbed "musicking."[103] According to Small (1998, 9), "to music is to take part, in any capacity, in a musical performance, whether by performing, by listening, by rehearsing or practicing, by providing material for performance (what is called composing), or by dancing." For Wittgenstein, these are all occasions for evincing musical

---

[103] I should note that this is part and parcel of what can be called Wittgenstein's "doer's perspective" on aesthetics. For Wittgenstein, the objects of aesthetic considerations are not just objects of representation, but the agents of aesthetic experience are actively engaged with the objects. These objects are part of how we live in the world. The "doer's perspective" is precisely the onset for making illuminating comparisons (see Section 3.3 above). I am indebted to an anonymous referee for this point.

understanding by way of characterizing. I know that someone understands a piece of music, says Wittgenstein (MS 153b, 60v-61r),

> if he can say, for every note, how it has to be played, if he can set the tempo for each measure. Eventually also, if he can justify this by saying: it's just like when someone says ... or: that corresponds to this dance step, or: that's the answer to that, or by considering the piece in Schenker's way. Or by saying: that has to be played like a waltz, or: this is serious, but not sad.

Here the idea of musical understanding displaces that of musical meaning.

Wittgenstein resisted the idea that musical meaning is explicable in terms of a relation between music and something else; that, in this sense, music is about something in the world (or in ourselves). Wittgenstein's insight that musical meaning is an internal relation – a relation that denies the separateness of the things it joins – sharply distinguishes him from contemporary discussions of musical meaning, which often still hinge upon whether music is somehow related to extra-musical emotions and whether this might have anything to do with the value of music. For Wittgenstein, we can have no idea what musical meaning might be unless we have some grasp of what distinguishes the one who hears with under-standing from the one who merely hears. This is the crux of the notion of musicality, which has established itself as a philosophical driving force for Wittgenstein from the very beginning of his career, strikingly even before the time of the *Tractatus*.

Wittgenstein's notion of a reciprocal action, which obtains between music and language, evinced the thrust of his mature language-as-music simile. It capitalizes on a conception of music as a deed, as something that people do, as an ever-open invitation to learn, listen, and play. It recovers the sense in which musical performances are not merely subservient to the musical work. Rather, musical works exist so that performers will have something to perform (although they can surely do without it as is the case in non-Western musical traditions, for example). Mutual tuning-in relationships are prior to the score, or anything mental or otherwise disembodied that the score is alleged to enshrine, and they enliven the score. Wittgenstein's treatment of examples for mechanical means of music reproduction, such as the pianola, settles the case. And he (CV, 54 [47]) openly contended that melodies (which could be regarded for the sake of argument as embryonic "musical works," often taken formally as mere sequences of notes and key changes) are "steps along a path that leads from something you would not call a melody to something else that you again would not call one" – they are moves in a practice of characterizing, that is, making perspicuous, displaying, unveiling, bringing out and setting forth.

It is difficult to demarcate Wittgenstein's paradigm shift from within a musical culture that has become dominated by the ideal of literate performance, and more so when viewed from the vantage point of a contemporary philosophy of music, whose theories predominantly remain premised upon the conceptual primacy of "the work" and whose origins (deeply rooted in the inner/outer picture that Wittgenstein was adamant to dissolve) had made it inimical to Wittgenstein's philosophical insights. Within such a context, the word "music" conveniently translates to either "language" or "musical works." The former is deflected by the directionality of Wittgenstein's language-as-music simile. The second generates in turn a host of ontological questions concerning *how* and *where* such works exist. While Wittgenstein makes numerous references to specific works of music (often taking the opportunity to voice his cultured taste), he is not concerned with such questions at all.

Furthermore, from within the prevailing paradigm, the perennial question, "What is the meaning of music?" tends to morph into quite a different one: "What is the meaning of this work (or these works) of music?" The second makes it necessary to search for external relations between "the work" and "the world" that we could explicate independently in generalized terms. Here, theories abound still. Yet, Wittgenstein clearly resists the trap of reification: he is unwilling to buy into thinking in terms of abstractions or ideals that supposedly underpin and suffuse the actions. He reverts from the second question to the first, and then expunges it in his "tale of two paradigms."

Wittgenstein's emphasis on mutual tuning-in relationships serves to undercut a tendency among philosophers of music (of pronounced empirical bent) to cave in to what Sloboda (1986) called the "pharmaceutical model" of musical experience. This is the idea that listeners "are the passive recipient of musical stimuli which have the psychological effect they do because of the way that the human brain is constructed, on the one hand, and the way that music is constructed, on the other" (Sloboda 1986, 319). Wittgenstein mocks this idea, that music is some sort of trigger, on countless occasions for its confusion of causes and reasons in aesthetics, its artistic and cultural inanity, its dogmatic reliance on the inner/outer picture, and its equally dogmatic reliance on the conviction that our psychological concepts are semantically rigid and determinate, which Wittgenstein's discussion of "patterns of life" was designed to dismantle.

From Wittgenstein's perspective, the "pharmaceutical model" needlessly restricts our way of thinking about musical experience in that it overlooks the richly interactive, explorative, world-engaged, embodied, and embedded nature of musical experience.[104] It belittles the role of the listeners: how they listen, and how they actively engage with music to forge relationships and shared

---

[104] This is in accord with recent interpretations of enactivism in the later Wittgenstein. See, e.g., Hutto (2013) and Moyal-Sharrock (2013).

experiences. The "pharmaceutical model" not only ignores this active dimension of musical experience, it also overlooks the ways that music and musicality are deeply embedded in everyday life, informing and shaping our relationships and communicative practices. This is precisely the onus of Wittgenstein's intrinsic shift.

The fact that Wittgenstein was so consistently adamant, as evident already in his letter to Koder (LK, 37–38), about self-reorienting and self-knowing that comes with characterizing in mutual tuning-in relationships – how characterization can change one and all in return – makes him a forefather to what Alva Noë (2023) calls "an aesthetics for the entanglement."[105] Noë argues that what distinguishes us as human beings is that our simplicity is complex and fluid. We cannot sharply distinguish between what we do by nature, or by habit, from the second-order ways that we think about and experience our own performance. In humankind the two levels are entangled; there is no first order without the second, and the second loops down and affects the first. We are entangled, and we ourselves are products of this entanglement.

Wittgenstein's notion of the verticality of interrelated language games is a looping down of musical gestures that affects its presupposed language games in return. Thus, says Wittgenstein (CV, 59 [52]), "the theme is a *new part* of our language, it becomes incorporated in it; we learn a new *gesture* [*sic*]." This is the onset for the aesthetic predicament, according Noë (2023, 97): "We are not fixed, stable, defined, and known; the very act of trying to bring ourselves, our consciousness, our worlds, into focus, reorganizes and changes us. We are an aesthetic phenomenon." Here is Wittgenstein (CV, 83 [73]) again: "This musical phrase is a gesture for me. It creeps into my life. I *make* it my own."[106] What is central in Wittgenstein's aesthetics for the entanglement, which is also to say, what makes Wittgenstein's view so different from customary philosophy of music, is precisely its focus on what Noë (2023, 169–175) calls "the aesthetic work."

Aesthetic work is the achievement of a perspicuous representation by means of coming up with illuminating comparisons. It is the effortful reorientation of ourselves, enacting ourselves in relation to others in the world, so that we may attain game incorrigibility, and, in that sense, see and know. This is at the heart of the mutually transformative tuning-in relationships, which so many of Wittgenstein's remarks on music unfurl, hence at the heart of his master simile of language-as-music. It is the labor of what Noë calls "achieving the object" and Floyd (2018a, 2018b) explains in terms of Wittgenstein's deepening humanized emphasis on characterization, which evinces his career-long pull

---

[105] Noë acknowledges this in chapter ten of his book.   [106] My emphasis.

away from Russell's notion of acquaintance as a singular, immediate, incorrigible, direct mental contact with objects or universals, and back onto everyday life, where being acquainted with a person "requires comportment, culture, conversation: looking, conversing, being corrected, and listening, fallibly, *to* the person" (2018b, 68). Such work is patently risky. As Noë (2023, 168) points out, "it requires effort and curiosity; it requires looking and interrogation; it requires thought. It requires a kind of labor. Typically it also requires other people; that is, the natural setting for most robust aesthetic encounters with what there is around you (an artwork, or a sunset) is social." This is the advent of making music together. Yet, this means that Wittgenstein's aesthetics for the entanglement rushes in, fully aware, where philosophers of music, who normally offer thoughtful consideration to matters of aesthetic judgment, fear to tread. For the "aesthetic work" is antecedent to the making of such judgments. Aesthetic work is all about the found depths along an unending, indeterminate journey of creatively bringing the world into focus.

It is here, I find, that Wittgenstein's paradigm shift, in its twofold form, shows itself in its full incommensurable glory vis-à-vis ongoing debates in contemporary analytic philosophy of music concerning a topic, which I highlighted in the preceding sections as Wittgenstein's ultimate philosophical response to the proclivities of German Romanticism – the thorny question concerning the profundity of music.

I argued elsewhere (Guter 2019c) that the current debate concerning musical profundity, which began with Peter Kivy's seminal book *Music Alone* (1990), is structured around, and regulated by the "container" metaphor of musical depth, which was handed over from German Romanticism. The debate emerged complete with a notion of depth as vertical progress toward a purported core, and a notion of hiddenness, suggesting the distinctive Romantic baggage and endemic tension between knowability and unknowability, concerning the purportedly indeterminate, inexhaustible nature of whatever is said to be contained within pertaining to the celebrated power of music to carry over and reveal things about human nature or about our place in the world. Kivy's unrepentant skepticism about musical profundity, and the responses that it elicited over the passing three decades, invariably reveal that the ensuing contemporary debate swallowed the Romantic framing of the discourse hook, line, and sinker, complete with all these endemic tensions.

It is said that a work of music can be said to be profound, only if it could be shown that the work is about something profound in itself, or that whatever the work says about its purported subject matter is in itself profound, and that somehow all this is contained within the work, awaits being unearthed, recognized, evoked, recollected, or at least apprehended nondiscursively. Thus, the idea of aboutness – in the sense of possessing the possibility of a subject matter – marks the metaphorical orientation of depth for the "container" metaphor, which regulates the prevailing debate concerning musical profundity.

Given his formalist stance, Kivy was firm in his debunking of the aboutness criterion. "[F]or a work to be profound," he (Kivy 1990, 203–204) wrote,

> it must fulfill at least three conditions: it must be able to be "about" (that is, it must possess the possibility of a subject matter); it must be about something profound (which is to say, something of abiding interest or importance to human beings); it must treat its profound subject matter in some exemplary way or other adequate to that subject matter (function, in other words, at some acceptably high aesthetic level).

Yet since, as he maintained, instrumental music is a quasi-syntactic structure, without meaning, reference, or representational features, it cannot be about anything, and while some of its features are expressive, music is still not about the emotions.

Furthermore, he argued that even if we grant that music satisfies the aboutness criterion by saying that music is about the very possibilities of musical sound itself, we eventually run into vicious circularity. Short of finding a way to construe musical sound itself as a profound subject matter independently of its containing profound musical works, we can only say that "there are profound musical works only if musical sound is a profound subject matter; musical sound is a profound subject matter only if there are profound musical works" (Kivy 1990, 216–217). Ultimately, Kivy reluctantly gave in to the force of the radical skeptical conclusion that since so-called absolute music fails to meet these criteria it cannot rightly be called profound.

Kivy's skepticism about musical profundity has not been left unanswered. Criticism focused on his formulation of the aboutness criterion for being too restrictive, essentially propositional, gravitating toward systematic or conventional relations of reference or denotation, or misconstruing its subject matter.[107] Indeed, Kivy seems to have created an acute need within the circle of analytic aesthetics to rescue musical profundity from skeptical oblivion by repairing the aboutness criterion for music. Kivy's critics struggled to find nonsemantic means of exhibiting or presenting some profound content in musical works, thereby loosening the strong semantic commitment to the aboutness criterion, which has been mandated by Kivy.[108]

---

[107] See Levinson 1992, White 1992, Ridley 1995, Robinson 2000, Davies 2002, Dodd 2014, Hulatt 2017. Kivy responded in Kivy (1997, 2003).
[108] For detailed discussion see Guter (2019c).

In the present context, it is important to point out the contours that Kivy's argument lends to the ensuing debate concerning the profundity of music. He was adamant in his attempt to remove from that "container" any metaphorical orientation of depth, as epitomized by the aboutness criterion. For Kivy, no verticality was allowed. He rejected the very idea of content (nontrivial knowledge of something) qua the interior dimension of the "container"; yet he ended up envisioning a container with no core. At the end of *Music Alone*, when, perplexed by the fatal circularity of the attempt to construe musical sound as the subject of profound musical works, Kivy turns on his heels at the edge of the abyss, unable to see any further. Skepticism was for him a way out of the inevitable implosion of the "container" metaphor of depth.

Here Wittgenstein's logical reorientation of verticality as the depth of a journey, with its ineliminable emphasis on unending "aesthetic work," shows its mettle. For in his "tale of two paradigms," the two paradigms are internally related. The aboutness criterion, on the other hand, presupposes the separateness of music from an extra-musical world. In this sense, Kivy's defiant position can be seen as a fully realized philosophy of music held captive by a picture of musical meaning as a relation between music and something else. Drawing the most consistent conclusions from the original Romantic construal of musical profundity in terms of the unsearchable core of a "musical container," Kivy literally pushed it all the way to the breaking point, showing that it cannot sustain its own weight once whittled down by skepticism concerning a purported semantic link that obtains between music and human life.

Yet from the perspective of Wittgenstein's paradigm shift this is a nonissue. The threat of vicious circularity is symptomatic of thinking of musical sound apart from gesture – that is, apart from what Wittgenstein considered to be the preconditions, and the lived, embodied realities, of musical intelligibility. Circularity would be fatal only if one seeks out provable knowledge. Surely, we can let go of this picture, if knowing human beings has no room for the concept of doubt and the attainment of moments of game incorrigibility are of our own deliberate making. Letting go would amount to affirming that musical profundity is internally related to human life and spread across its filigree-shaped patterns which we traverse all-too-fallibly as we make music, engaging creatively, intellectually, and physically in this culturally embedded, embodied activity involving organized sound. This is what Cavell (2022, 254) calls, following Wittgenstein, "understanding without meaning," suggesting "a particular form of communication, of revelation, one in which the demand for expression is put to the test." That we may still be inclined at times to say that the music expresses itself (even if is not "about itself") is not a pronouncement of a tautology, or some vicious circularity, but an acknowledgment that we have landed on a steppingstone, and that the creative journey in language that lies ahead forever remains unending and incomplete.

References

Works Cited by Abbreviation

BB   Wittgenstein, L. (1958). *The Blue and Brown Books*. Oxford: Blackwell.

BT   Wittgenstein, L. (2005). *The Big Typescript: TS 213*. C. G. Luckhardt and M. A. E. Aue, eds. Oxford: Blackwell.

CV   Wittgenstein, L. (1998 [1980]). *Culture and Value*. 1998 ed. by G. H. von Wright, H. Nyman, and A. Pichler, eds.; P. Winch, tr. 1980 ed. by G. H. von Wright and H. Nyman eds.; P. Winch, tr. Oxford: Blackwell.

LC   Wittgenstein, L. (1966). *Lectures and Conversations on Aesthetics, Psychology and Religious Belief*. C. Barrett, ed. Berkeley: University of California Press.

LK   Wittgenstein, L. and Koder, R. (2000). *Wittgenstein und die Musik: Ludwig Wittgenstein und Rudolf Koder Briefwechsel*. M. Alber, ed. Innsbruck: Haymon.

LO   Wittgenstein, L. (1973). *Letters to C. K. Ogden*. G. H. von Wright, ed. Oxford: Basil Blackwell.

LR   Wittgenstein, L. and Richards, B. (2023). *"I Think of You Constantly with Love ..."*: *Briefwechsel Ludwig Wittgenstein – Ben Richards 1946–1951*. A. Schmidt, ed. Innsbruck: Haymon.

LWI   Wittgenstein, L. (1982). *Last Writings on the Philosophy of Psychology: Preliminary Studies for Part 2 of Philosophical Investigations*, Vol. 1. G. H. von Wright and H. Nyman, eds.; C. G. Luckhardt and M. A. E. Aue, trs. Chicago: The University of Chicago Press.

LWII   Wittgenstein, L. (1993). *Last Writings on the Philosophy of Psychology: The Inner and the Other*, Vol. 2. G. H. von Wright and H. Nyman, eds.; C. G. Luckhardt and M. A. E. Aue, trs. Oxford: Blackwell.

MT   Wittgenstein, L. (2003). "Movements of Thought: Diaries, 1930–1932, 1936–1937." In J. C. Klagge and A. Nordmann, eds., *Ludwig Wittgenstein: Public and Private Occasions*. Lanham: Rowman & Littlefield, 3–251.

NB   Wittgenstein, L. (1961). *Notebooks 1914–1916*. G. H. von Wright and G. E. M. Anscombe, eds.; G. E. M. Anscombe, tr. Oxford: Blackwell.

OC   Wittgenstein, L. (1972). *On Certainty*. New York: Harper.

PG   Wittgenstein, L. (1974). *Philosophical Grammar*. R. Rhees, ed.; A. Kenny, tr. Berkeley: University of California Press.

PI   Wittgenstein, L. (2009 [1958]). *Philosophical Investigations*. Revised 4th ed., P. M. S. Hacker and J. Schulte, eds.; G. E. M. Anscombe, P. M. S. Hacker, and J. Schulte, trs. 2nd ed., G. E. M. Anscombe and R. Rhees, eds.; G. E. M. Anscombe, tr. Oxford: Blackwell.

PPF   Wittgenstein, L. (2009). "Philosophy of Psychology: A Fragment." Previously Known as Part II of the *Philosophical Investigations*. In *Philosophical Investigations*, 182–244.

PR   Wittgenstein, L. (1975). *Philosophical Remarks*. Rush Rhees, ed.; R. Hargreaves and R. White, trs. Oxford: Blackwell.

PT   Wittgenstein, L. (1971). *Prototractatus: An Early Version of Tractatus Logico-Philosophicus*. B. F. McGuinness, T. Nyberg, and G. H. von Wright, eds.; D. F. Pears and B. F. McGuinness, trs. London: Routledge & Kegan Paul.

RFM   Wittgenstein, L. (1998). *Remarks on the Foundations of Mathematics*. G. E. M. Anscombe, R. Rhees, and G. H. von Wright, eds.; G. E. M. Anscombe, tr. Oxford: Blackwell.

RPPI   Wittgenstein, L. (1980). *Remarks on the Philosophy of Psychology*, Vol. 1. G. E. M. Anscombe and G. H. von Wright, eds.; G. E. M. Anscombe, tr. Oxford: Blackwell.

RPPII   Wittgenstein, L. (1980). *Remarks on the Philosophy of Psychology*, Vol. 2. G. H. von Wright and H. Nyman, eds.; C. G. Luckhardt and M. A. E. Aue, trs. Chicago: The University of Chicago Press.

TLP   Wittgenstein, L. (1995). *Tractatus Logico-Philosophicus*. C. K. Ogden, tr. London: Routledge.

WLA   Wittgenstein, L. (2001). *Wittgenstein's Lectures: Cambridge, 1932–1935: From the Notes of Alice Ambrose and Margaret Macdonald*. A. Ambrose, ed. Amherst: Prometheus.

WLM   Wittgenstein, L. (2016). *Wittgenstein: Lectures, Cambridge 1930–1933: From the Notes of G. E. Moore*. D. Stern, B. Rogers, and G. Citron, eds. Cambridge: Cambridge University Press.

WVC   Wittgenstein, L. and Weismann, F. (2003). *The Voices of Wittgenstein: The Vienna Circle*. G. Baker, ed. London: Routledge.

WS Wittgenstein, L. (2019). *Wittgenstein Source*. A. Pichler and J. Wang, eds. www.wittgensteinsource.org.

Z Wittgenstein, L. (1967). *Zettel*. G. E. M. Anscombe and G. H. von Wright, eds.; G. E. M. Anscombe, tr. Berkeley: University of California Press.

Secondary Sources

Ahonen, H. (2005). "Wittgenstein and the Conditions of Musical Communication." *Philosophy* 80 (4), 513–529.

Allen, R. and Turvey, R. (2001). *Wittgenstein, Theory and the Arts*. London: Routledge.

Almén, B. (1996). "Prophets of the Decline: The Worldviews of Heinrich Schenker and Oswald Spengler." *Indiana Theory Review* 17, 1–24.

Appelqvist, H. (2019). "Wittgenstein and Formalism: A Case Revisited." *Ápeiron: Estudios defilosofía* 10, 9–27.

Appelqvist, H. (2023). *Wittgenstein and Aesthetics*. Cambridge: Cambridge University Press.

Arbo, A. (2013). *Entendre comme: Wittgenstein et l'esthétique musicale*. Paris: Hermann.

Baz, A. (2000). "What's the Point of Seeing Aspects?" *Philosophical Investigations* 23 (3), 97–121.

Baz, A. (2020). *Wittgenstein on Aspect Perception*. Cambridge: Cambridge University Press.

Bolton, T. L. (1894). "Rhythm." *American Journal of Psychology* 6, 145–238.

Bowie, A. (2007). *Music, Philosophy, and Modernity*. Cambridge: Cambridge University Press.

Cavell, S. (1979). *The Claim of Reason: Wittgenstein, Skepticism, Morality, and Tragedy*. Oxford: Oxford University Press.

Cavell, S. (1996). "Declining Decline." In S. Mulhall, ed., *The Cavell Reader*. Oxford: Blackwell, 321–352.

Cavell, S. (2022). *Here and There: Sites of Philosophy*. N. Bauer, A. Crary, and S. Laugier, eds. Cambridge, MA: Harvard University Press.

Cook, N. (1989). "Schenker's Theory of Music as Ethics." *The Journal of Musicology* 7, 415–439.

Cooke, D. (1964). *The Language of Music*. London: Oxford University Press.

Davies, S. (2002). "Profundity in Instrumental Music." *British Journal of Aesthetics* 42 (4), 343–356.

Davies, S. (2011). "Analytic Philosophy and Music." In T. Gracyk and A. Kania, eds., *The Routledge Companion to Philosophy and Music*. Oxford: Oxford University Press, 294–304.

Dodd, J. (2014). "The Possibility of Profound Music." *British Journal of Aesthetics* 54 (3), 299–322.

Drury, M. O'C. (2017). *The Selected Writings of Maurice O'Connor Drury: On Wittgenstein, Philosophy, Religion, and Psychiatry*. J. Hayes, ed. London: Bloomsbury.

Eggers, K. (2014). *Ludwig Wittgenstein als Musikphilosoph*. Freiburg im Breisgau: Karl Alber.

Engelmann, M. L. (2013). "Wittgenstein's 'Most Fruitful Ideas' and Sraffa." *Philosophical Investigations* 36, 155–178.

Floyd, J. (2010). "On Being Surprised: Wittgenstein on Aspect-Perception, Logic, and Mathematics." In W. Day and V. J. Krebs, eds., *Seeing Wittgenstein Anew*. Cambridge: Cambridge University Press, 314–337.

Floyd, J. (2016). "Chains of Life: Turing, Lebensform, and the Emergence of Wittgenstein's Later Style." *Nordic Wittgenstein Review* 5 (2), 7–89.

Floyd, J. (2017). "The Fluidity of Simplicity: Philosophy, Mathematics, Art." In R. Kossak and P. Ording, eds., *Simplicity: Ideals of Practice in Mathematics and the Arts*. New York: Springer, 153–175.

Floyd, J. (2018a). "Aspects of Aspects." In H. Sluga and D. Stern, eds., *The Cambridge Companion to Wittgenstein*, 2nd ed. New York: Cambridge University Press, 361–388.

Floyd, J. (2018b). "Lebensformen: Living Logic." In C. Martin, ed., *Language, Form(s) of Life, and Logic*. Berlin: De Gruyter, 59–92.

Goehr, L. (2016). "Improvising Impromptu or, What to Do with a Broken String." In G. Lewis and B. Piekut, eds., *Oxford Handbook of Critical Improvisation Studies*, Vol. 1. New York: Oxford University Press, 458–480.

Guter, E. (2011). "A Surrogate for the Soul: Wittgenstein and Schoenberg." In E. De Pellegrin, ed., *Interactive Wittgenstein: Essays in Memory of Georg Henrik von Wright*. Synthese Library, Vol. 349. Dordrecht: Springer, 109–152.

Guter, E. (2015). "The Good, the Bad, and the Vacuous: Wittgenstein on Modern and Future Musics." *The Journal of Aesthetics and Art Criticism* 73 (4), 425–439.

Guter, E. (2017). "Wittgenstein on Musical Depth and Our Knowledge of the Humankind." In G. Hagberg, ed., *Wittgenstein on Aesthetic Understanding*. Cham: Palgrave Macmillan, 217–247.

Guter, E. (2019a). "'A Small, Shabby Crystal, yet a Crystal': A Life of Music in Wittgenstein's *Denkbewegungen*." In I. Somavilla, C. Hamphries, and B. Sieradzka-Baziur, eds., *Wittgenstein's Denkbewegungen. Diaries 1930–*

1932/1936–1937: Interdisciplinary Perspectives. Innsbruck: StudienVerlag, 83–112.

Guter, E. (2019b). "Measure for Measure: Wittgenstein's Critique of the Augustinian Picture of Music." In H. Appelqvist, ed., *Wittgenstein and the Limits of Language*. London: Routledge, 245–269.

Guter, E. (2019c). "Musical Profundity: Wittgenstein's Paradigm Shift." *Ápeiron: Estudios de filosofía* 10, 41–58.

Guter, E. (2020). "The Philosophical Significance of Wittgenstein's Experiments on Rhythm, Cambridge 1912–13." *Estetika: The European Journal of Aesthetics* 57 (1), 28–43.

Guter, E. (2023a). "Musicking as Knowing Human Beings." In C. Carmona, D. Perez-Chico, and C. Tejedor, eds., *Intercultural Understanding after Wittgenstein*. London: Anthem, 77–91.

Guter, E. (2023b). "Wittgenstein in the Laboratory: Pre-Tractatus Seeds of Wittgenstein's Post-Tractatus Aesthetics." In A. Pichler, E. Heinrich-Ramharter, and F. Stadler, eds., *100 Years of Tractatus Logico-Philosophicus – 70 Years after Wittgenstein's Death: A Critical Assessment*, Papers of the 44th International Wittgenstein Symposium. Kirchberg am Wechsel: Austrian Ludwig Wittgenstein Society. https://symposium.alws.at/#/article/511c6b7a-b66f-4793-9e46-88e35735905d.

Guter, E. (2024). "Carl Stumpf and the Curious Incident of Music in Wittgenstein's *Tractatus*." *Archiv für Geschichte der Philosophie*. https://doi.org/10.1515/agph-2021-0141

Guter, E. (Forthcoming). "Cavell's Odd Couple: Wittgenstein and Schoenberg." In D. LaRocca, ed., *Music with Stanley Cavell in Mind*. London: Bloomsbury.

Guter, E. and Guter, I. (2023). "Thinking through Music: Wittgenstein's Use of Musical Notation." *The Journal of Aesthetics and Art Criticism* 81 (3), 348–362. https://doi.org/10.1093/jaac/kpad033.

Hagberg, G. (2011). "Wittgenstein's Philosophical Investigations, Linguistic Meaning and Music." *Paragraph* 34 (3), 388–405.

Hagberg, G. (2014). "Wittgenstein's Aesthetics." *The Stanford Encyclopedia of Philosophy (Fall 2014 ed.)*, E. N. Zalta, ed. https://plato.stanford.edu/archives/fall2014/entries/wittgenstein-aesthetics.

Hagberg, G. (2017). "Wittgenstein, Music, and the Philosophy of Culture." In G. Hagberg, ed., *Wittgenstein on Aesthetic Understanding*. Basingstoke: Palgrave Macmillan, 61–98.

Hanslick, E. (2018). *On the Musically Beautiful*. New York: Oxford University Press.

Hark, M. ter (1990). *Beyond the Inner and the Outer: Wittgenstein's Philosophy of Psychology.* Dordrecht: Kluwer.

Hintikka, M. B. and Hintikka, J. (1986). *Investigating Wittgenstein.* Oxford: Basil Blackwell.

Hintikka, M. B. and Hintikka, J. (1996). "Different Language Games in Wittgenstein." In J. Hintikka, *Wittgenstein: Half-Truths and One-and-a-Half-Truths. Selected Papers 1.* Dordrecht: Kluwer, 335–343.

Hui, A. (2013). *The Psychophysical Ear: Musical Experiments, Experimental Sounds, 1840-1910.* Cambridge, MA: Harvard University Press.

Hulatt, O. (2017). "'Pure Showing' and Anti-humanist Musical Profundity." *British Journal of Aesthetics* 57 (2), 195–210.

Husserl, E. (1964). *The Phenomenology of Internal Time-Consciousness.* Bloomington: Indiana University Press.

Hutto, D. D. (2013). "Enactivism from a Wittgensteinian Point of View." *American Philosophical Quarterly* 50 (3), 281–302.

Joyce, J. (2000). *Ulysses.* London: Penguin.

Kittler, F. A. (1999). *Gramophone, Film, Typewriter.* Stanford: Stanford University Press.

Kivy, P. (1990). *Music Alone: Philosophical Reflections on the Purely Musical Experience.* Ithaca: Cornell University Press.

Kivy, P. (1997). *Philosophies of Arts: An Essay in Differences.* New York: Cambridge University Press.

Kivy, P. (2003). "Another Go at Musical Profundity: Stephen Davies and the Game of Chess." *British Journal of Aesthetics* 43 (4), 401–411.

Kramer, L. (2012). *Expression and Truth: On the Music of Knowledge.* Berkley: The University of California Press.

Kursell, J. (2018). "Carl Stumpf and the Beginnings of Research in Musicality." In H. Honing, ed., *The Origins of Musicality.* Cambridge, MA: Harvard University Press, 323–346.

Kursell, J. (2019). "From Tone to Tune – Carl Stumpf and the Violin." *19th Century Music* 43 (2), 121–139.

Lakoff, G. and Johnson, M. (1980). *Metaphors We Live by.* Chicago: The University of Chicago Press.

Langer, S. K. (1953). *Feeling and Form.* London: Routledge and Kegan Paul.

Lerdahl, F. and Jackendoff, R. (1983). *A Generative Theory of Tonal Music.* Cambridge, MA: MIT Press.

Levinson, J. (1992). "Musical Profundity Misplaced." *Journal of Aesthetics and Art Criticism* 50 (1), 58–60.

Levinson, J. (1997). *Music in the Moment.* Ithaca: Cornell University Press.

Lewis, P. B. (2004). *Wittgenstein, Aesthetics and Philosophy*. Aldershot: Ashgate.

McGuinness, B. (1988). *Wittgenstein, a Life: Young Ludwig, 1889–1921*. Berkeley: University of California Press.

Monk, R. (1990). *Ludwig Wittgenstein: The Duty of Genius*. New York: Free Press.

Moyal-Sharrock, D. (2013). "Wittgenstein's Razor: The Cutting Edge of Enactivism." *American Philosophical Quarterly* 50 (3), 263–279.

Mulhall, S. (1990). *On Being in the World: Wittgenstein and Heidegger on Seeing Aspects*. London: Routledge.

Myers, C. S. (2013). *A Text-Book of Experimental Psychology, with Laboratory Exercises*, 2 vols. Cambridge: Cambridge University Press.

Noë, A. (2023). *The Entanglement: How Art and Philosophy Make Us What We Are*. Princeton: Princeton University Press.

Pinsent, D. (1990). *A Portrait of Wittgenstein as a Young Man: From the Diary of David Hume Pinsent 1912–1914*. G. H. von Wright, ed. Oxford: Blackwell.

Potter, M. (2008). *Wittgenstein's Notes on Logic*. Oxford: Oxford University Press.

Ridley, A. (1995). "Profundity in Music." In A. Neill and A. Ridley, eds., *Arguing about Art: Contemporary Philosophical Debates*. New York: McGraw-Hill, 260–272.

Rilke, R. M. (1961). "Primal Sound." In *Selected Works*, Vol. 1. Prose. G. C. Houston, tr. New York: New Directions, 51–56.

Robinson, J. (2000). "Review of Philosophy of Arts: An Essay in Differences, by Peter Kivy." *Philosophical Review* 109, 138–141.

Schoenberg, A. (1999). *Fundamentals of Music Composition*. London: Faber & Faber.

Schopenhauer, A. (1969). *The World as Will and Representation*, Vols. I and II. E. F. J. Payne, tr. New York: Dover.

Schorske, C. E. (1999). *Thinking with History: Explorations in the Passage to Modernism*. Princeton: Princeton University Press.

Schütz, A. (1951). "Making Music Together: A Study in Social Relationship." *Social Research* 18 (1), 76–97.

Scruton, R. (1999). *The Aesthetics of Music*. Oxford: Oxford University Press.

Scruton, R. (2004). "Wittgenstein and the Understanding of Music." *British Journal of Aesthetics* 44 (1), 1–9.

Sloboda, J. (1986). *The Musical Mind: The Cognitive Psychology of Music*. Oxford: Clarendon.

Small, C. (1998). *Musicking: The Meanings of Performing and Listening.* Middlebury: Wesleyan University Press.

Snarrenberg, R. (1997). *Schenker's Interpretative Practice.* Cambridge: Cambridge University Press.

Soulez, A. (2006). "Time, Music and Grammar: When Understanding and Performing What is Understood Are Two Facets of the Same Action." In F. Stadler and M. Stöltzner, eds., *Time and History: Zeit und Geschichte.* Frankfurt: Ontos Verlag, 585–599.

Soulez, A. (2012). *Au fil du motif – autour de Wittgenstein et la musique.* Paris: Delatour.

Spengler, O. (1939). *The Decline of the West.* New York: Alfred A. Knopf.

Stern, D. (1991). "The 'Middle Wittgenstein': From Logical Atomism to Practical Holism." *Synthese* 87, 203–226.

Sterrett, S. G. (2005). "Pictures of Sounds: Wittgenstein on Gramophone Records and the Logic of Depiction." *Studies in the History and Philosophy of Science* 36, 351–362.

Stumpf, C. (1883). *Tonpsychologie*, Vol. 2. Leipzig: Hirzel.

Stumpf, C. (2012). *The Origins of Music.* Oxford: Oxford University Press.

Sully, J. (1886). "Review of Musikpsychologie in England." *Mind* 11 (44), 580–585.

Szabados, B. (2006). "Wittgenstein and Musical Formalism." *Philosophy* 81, 649–658.

Szabados, B. (2014). *Wittgenstein as Philosophical Tone-Poet: Philosophy and Music in Dialogue.* Amsterdam: Rodopi.

Taylor, C. (1996). *Sources of the Self: The Making of the Modern Identity.* Cambridge, MA: Harvard University Press.

Tejedor, C. (2015). "Tractarian Form as the Precursor to Forms of Life." *Nordic Wittgenstein Review*, Special Issue: Wittgenstein and Forms of Life, 83–110.

Valentine, C. W. (1962). *The Experimental Psychology of Beauty.* London: Methuen.

Wackenroder, W. H. (1971). *Confessions and Fantasies.* University Park: The Pennsylvania State University Press.

White, D. A. (1992). "Toward a Theory of Profundity in Music." *Journal of Aesthetics and Art Criticism* 50 (1), 23–34.

Woodrow, H. (1909). "A Quantitative Study of Rhythm." *Archives of Psychology* 14, 1–66.

Wright, G. H. von (1982). "Ludwig Wittgenstein in Relation to His Times." In B. McGuinness, ed., *Wittgenstein and His Times*. Chicago: The University of Chicago Press.

Wright, J. K. (2007). *Schoenberg, Wittgenstein and the Vienna Circle*, 2nd ed. Bern: Peter Lang.

Wundt, W. (1903). *Grundzüge der physiologischer Psychologie*, Vol. 3. Leipzig: Engelmann.

To Inbal, Eden, and Alma
with all my love

Cambridge Elements ≡

The Philosophy of Ludwig Wittgenstein

David G. Stern

University of Iowa

David G. Stern is a Professor of Philosophy and a Collegiate Fellow in the College of Liberal Arts and Sciences at the University of Iowa. His research interests include history of analytic philosophy, philosophy of language, philosophy of mind, and philosophy of science. He is the author of *Wittgenstein's Philosophical Investigations: An Introduction* (Cambridge University Press, 2004) and *Wittgenstein on Mind and Language* (Oxford University Press, 1995), as well as more than 50 journal articles and book chapters. He is the editor of *Wittgenstein in the 1930s: Between the 'Tractatus' and the 'Investigations'* (Cambridge University Press, 2018) and is also a co-editor of the *Cambridge Companion to Wittgenstein* (Cambridge University Press, 2nd edition, 2018), *Wittgenstein: Lectures, Cambridge 1930–1933, from the Notes of G. E. Moore* (Cambridge University Press, 2016) and *Wittgenstein Reads Weininger* (Cambridge University Press, 2004).

About the Series

This series provides concise and structured introductions to all the central topics in the philosophy of Ludwig Wittgenstein. The Elements are written by distinguished senior scholars and bright junior scholars with relevant expertise, producing balanced and comprehensive coverage of the full range of Wittgenstein's thought.

Cambridge Elements ≡

The Philosophy of Ludwig Wittgenstein

A full series listing is available at: www.cambridge.org/EPLW

Printed in the United States
by Baker & Taylor Publisher Services